INFORMING THE PEOPLE

Anthony James

London: HMSO

ISBN 0 11 702014 1

A CIP catalogue record for this book is available from the British Library.

Front cover: Reprinted from *Tunisia* (MoI/HMSO, 1944, for War Office)

Back cover: Reprinted from *The Royal Marines* (MoI/HMSO, 1944, for Admiralty

Chapter 1: Reprinted from *Persuading the People* (HMSO, 1993)

Chapter 2: Reprinted from *RAF Middle East* (MoI/HMSO, 1945)

Chapter 3: Reprinted from *The Royal Armoured Corps* (HMSO, 1945)

Chapter 4: Reprinted from *The Mediterranean Fleet* (MoI/HMSO, 1944)

Chapter 5: Reprinted from *The Metropolitan Police at War* (HMSO, 1947)

Chapter 6: Reprinted from *The Australian Army at War 1939–1944* (Australian Army Staff/HMSO, 1944)

Chapter 7: Reprinted from *The Battle of Britain* (MoI/HMSO, 1941)

Chapter 8: Reprinted from *Our Men in Korea* (CoI/HMSO, 1952)

CONTENTS

Acknowledgements

Author and publisher would like to thank the following for permission to reproduce illustrations: BBC for the cover of *BBC at War*; Froglets Publications (supported by Kent County Council, Arts and Libraries) for the cover of *Flying Bombs Over England*; Hodder & Stoughton Ltd (for the Society of Motor Manufacturers and Traders Ltd) for the cover of *Drive for Freedom*; Hutchinson & Co. (for London County Council) for the cover of *Fire Over London*; the Trustees of the Imperial War Museum, London.

I am also most grateful to Jack Wales and Ian Sayer, both of whom rendered valuable help with the harder-to-find later pamphlets.

JACQUELINE
(who died while this book was being written)

Thank you for so much love, encouragement and support,
that never wavered over so many years.

5 August 1932 – 6 March 1996

Chapter 1

Ministry of Information

The Birth of a Great Idea

A SECRET WEAPON?

In the late 1930s, the looming war threatened to be unlike any previous war in history. Germany had built the world's largest air force, and Stanley Baldwin, Britain's pre-war Prime Minister, had echoed the theory that 'the bomber will always get through'. Government and people, perhaps believing him too literally, anticipated skies blackened by armadas of aircraft raining bombs upon undefendable cities. Britannia would undoubtedly rule the waves – but not until first having found and destroyed hordes of Nazi U-boats – while the newly mechanised armies would scythe through Europe.

There would be 'blitz', and Fifth Columns, and war by propaganda, stretching morale to breaking point. Planning for modern war would have to include 'psychological arming' – keeping the combatants, who would now include the civilians, forewarned and informed. The Nazis had shown the way, with their Ministry of Volk Enlightenment – Dr Goebbels' Ministry of Propaganda. As a counter, Britain would need its own organisation, a Ministry of Information. After secret preparations, on Monday morning, 4 September 1939, it uncovered its nameplate and opened for business. It planned to use every device of the media to fight Hitler and his hordes.

Prominent among the methods to be used to inform the people upon the war's progress would be a series of 'pamphlets', published mainly by the Ministry of Information on behalf either of the Service Ministries or other Ministries responsible for aspects of conducting the war, with printing and distribution arranged by His Majesty's Stationery Office. In this context, the word 'pamphlet' was used in its dictionary sense of 'a small, usually unbound, treatise on a subject of current interest'. In fact, most publications in the series more nearly resemble short paperbacks, usually of sixty pages or longer, though a few appeared in large-page, magazine format.

For convenience, this series has since come to be known as 'WW2 HMSO Paperbacks' and at present it extends to some seventy selected titles, although the list is still open, and further research may result in more titles being added. It is important to stress, though, that by no means every Ministry of Information/ HM Stationery Office pamphlet qualifies for inclusion. Excluded are all those intended only to provide useful advice (for example, on war-affected aspects of daily life – cooking, sewing, growing vegetables, using transport, taking holidays, use of fuels, etc.), as well as those providing necessary instruction in entirely new areas of responsibility (air raid shelters, response to air attack and invasion, black-out preparations, anti-gas precautions, etc.). Also excluded are publications supporting occasional propaganda campaigns, intended only to influence opinion and enhance morale. Again, for convenience, these excluded (but nonetheless, fascinating) items have become known as the 'non-series pamphlets' – and there are several scores of titles, outnumbering the selected 'series' pamphlets that, because of their often ephemeral nature or less durably relevant content, have become quite rare.

The WW2 HMSO Paperback series is restricted to works which provide a contemporary official record of an aspect of the conduct and progress of the war – what has been succinctly described as 'a first draft of history'. These pamphlets represent Government's attempts not to ask, nor to instruct, but to inform. In other words, only those pamphlets which record contemporary history are considered to be within the series, while all those which merely advise or exhort are now thought of as outside it. All of the series' earlier titles were published in a cheap format at a low price, and distributed widely in order that the nation should have the chance to know, and generally to know quickly, what was going on; what was being done in its name with its money; and what outcomes were being sought or had been achieved. Every effort was taken to ensure that each pamphlet told the truth as it was known at the time. All are without benefit of hindsight or of the balance that can be achieved after the events, by comparison, analysis and research. Thus they 'tell it how it was' to be living through the times, hearing the explosions, sharing the hardships, and feeling the pain and the relief. Truly, a first draft of history.

An added bonus is that, although most pamphlets appeared anonymously, many were written by experienced authors of established reputation, who could write well and thus provide a graphic, lively and easily comprehensible story. These authors were provided with full facilities to compile their records and, whilst security might demand some excisions from the resulting manuscripts, or delay in publication, their only instruction was to seek the truth, and to tell what they found. The legacy is as fascinating and valuable to today's readers as it has already proved to be to the official and unofficial historians who have made extensive use of the material during the following half-century. The sceptical should remember that the pamphlets' authors, with serious and respectable reputations to protect, had every opportunity after the war to repudiate their work for the Ministry, or to qualify the record they left. None of them has done so. Several have written of these experiences in their autobiographies. None of them has cast any post-war reservation upon the reliability of their wartime texts, or of the spirit in which they were commissioned.

Before dealing with the publications themselves, and their authors, it would be as well to provide some background information upon the backrooms from which these WW2 HMSO Paperbacks emerged: the Ministry of Information (MoI), HM Stationery Office (HMSO), and the separate Service Ministries – the Air Ministry, the War Office, and the Admiralty.

There already exist excellent histories of the work of MoI (for example, 'Ministry of Morale' by Ian McLaine, published by George Allen & Unwin, 1979). Thus, it is not necessary to re-cover that ground. But it will be helpful at least to provide some feel for the situation in which our WW2 HMSO Paperbacks series was conceived, and of the difficulties which the department responsible for most of them experienced. An earlier Ministry of Information had been created during the later stages of WW1, but its function was very different from that adopted by its WW2 namesake. Indeed, when the devisers of the projected new ministry called for the archives of MoI Mark 1, they could not be found! It was necessary to make a clean start, unburdened by any legacy of an earlier war.

Although those concerned at the time were careful to avoid reference to it, it is impossible to believe that the evident success and drive of the Nazi Government's and Dr Josef Goebbels' Ministry of Propaganda in Berlin was not a factor in the decision to prepare for the birth of Britain's MoI Mark 2. Its planners envisaged for it several principal functions, one of which should be publishing to present the national cause properly, through what was later to become known as the Publications Division. The intention was that a prime duty of MoI should be to sustain home morale, 'psychologically arming' civilians by presenting Britain's case through control of news and propaganda issued to the public.

The decision that a Ministry of Information should be ready for business immediately upon the outbreak of war was taken as early as 1935, and a shadow MoI existed from that time. It comprised only a committee plus a handful of civil servants who remained full-time with their original departments but undertook some moonlighting (at peril both to their health and their careers), apparently unpaid. Thus, the shadow MoI had no legal establishment, no budget, no equipment, no premises. It existed only in secret and on sufferance. Unhappily, it suffered another, more serious disadvantage.

Very few of those involved in its creation believed that here was a task worth undertaking. Some were actively hostile, and tried to prevent its creation. It sprung into life, officially established although severely handicapped, on 4 September 1939, with the appointment of Lord MacMillan (a senior judge) as the first Minister of Information. Its early months were plagued by changes of mind, changes of direction, and changes amongst the senior officials – there were, for example, four Ministers of Information in less than two years. From the outset, the headquarters of the new ministry was housed in the gleaming white, modern skyscraper block of University of London. Still untarnished by the Capital's sooty atmosphere, it was inevitably symbolic of that fabled dwelling, the Ivory Tower. The potential for jokes at MoI's expense was infinite. Unfortunately, MoI's most obvious skill during its first two years of existence was its ability to make a fool of itself, and feed the wits with material.

It soon became widely condemned for inefficiency; for irritating Parliament, the public and the press; and for what were perceived as comic blunders, thus becoming an object of general ridicule. Within a short time, two books had been published criticising, amongst other things, the ineptitude of many appointments to its staff. In 1942, by which time it had largely got its act together, it suffered the renewed ignominy of being expertly satirised in Evelyn Waugh's novel, *Put Out More Flags*. Some months before, two of its most senior officials had wanted to resign, convinced that Goebbels would continue to run rings around MoI, while its Minister, Duff Cooper, had described it as, 'a miserable freak bred from an unnatural union ... There has been a real improvement [but] ... the Prime Minister is not really interested in propaganda and still less in information'. Kenneth Clark resigned in August 1941 and later expressed the opinion that MoI had, in his time, been a useless body, the war in no way affected if it had been dissolved, except for its censorship role.

Not surprisingly, the ministry officially responsible for morale at first had no discernible morale of its own. Many of its important posts had been filled by recruitment from outside the civil service – from what many have come to think of as 'the chattering classes'; intellectuals with theories and enthusiasms, but often without either expertise or even basic experience in the fields they were recruited to direct. It was a plague of amateurs, learning by the seats of their pants, without commitment to remain in the service, and often earning much of their income from outside sources. MoI had not been provided by its planners with any 'mission statement' beyond vaguely described responsibilities for public morale, government publicity, aspects of censorship, and to broker news from the Service Ministries. It was not provided with authority to enforce its decisions, and was not empowered to insist upon compliance with its publicity and censorship advice, either by the Services or by the press. At times, it had to fight for its very existence, and against the active dislike and suspicion of the Prime Minister.

Throughout this unhappy early period, it remained a laughing stock in Parliament, a joke amongst the public, the butt of comedians on the radio and on the stage. Unsurprisingly, most of its publications of this era made little impact, and hardly figure in the list of WW2 HMSO Paperbacks series. This rolling disaster was slowed, first by publication in early 1941 of a worldwide best-selling pamphlet and then, in July 1941, by the appointment of Brendan Bracken as Minister of Information. Bracken was a close, personal friend of Winston Churchill with both the freedom of 10 Downing Street (actually living there for a while) and almost unrestricted access to Churchill's presence and attention. He also had the guts to face up to the great man, and carry his challenges through to a finish; a quality denied to all three of his predecessors and to most of his Cabinet colleagues. From this point, MoI ceased meddling with morale, and came to credit the British people with having common sense, and being both calm and courageous – qualities which many of the class-blinkered higher officials had thought 'the masses' incapable of, suspecting them to be infirm of purpose and likely to turn defeatist unless hectored or cajoled by better-motivated masters. Bracken realised that the 'propaganda of events' had far greater impact on morale than even the most strenuous publicity campaign, and that there was a reservoir of public goodwill to be drawn upon. He was to turn MoI around, to give it a mission, and to invest it with authority and gravitas. He remained in office until MoI's winding-down at the end of the war in Europe. Inevitably then, all except the very first and the last few of WW2 HMSO Paperbacks series titles appeared during his stewardship.

Concurrent with these events, the Service Ministries were having troubles of their own, so far as their attitudes to news and publicity were concerned. The Air Ministry, the War Office and, particularly, the Admiralty had never shared the earlier Chamberlain Government's view that it was essential to keep the public informed upon the progress of the war, on a day-to-day basis. They believed that the instruction to tell the public was an irritating nuisance that got in the way of getting on with hostilities. Perhaps more relevantly, they were convinced that it was actively dangerous to release any news at all, because of the help it was liable to give to the enemy. It was the case that a great deal of useful intelligence was gained from analysis of German broadcasts and newspapers, and the British Services were always anxious that the compliment should not be returned. The Air Ministry and the War Office were eventually enticed out into the sunlight, but the Admiralty, for long a firm advocate of compulsory censorship and no news releases, continued to try to hide behind its smokescreen for rather longer.

It is tempting to believe that what initiated the change might have been MoI's spectacular success with the first title in WW2 HMSO Paperbacks series, for a change does indeed become evident from that time, Spring 1941. That is probably an over-simplification, though, of an undoubtedly complex situation. It is to MoI's credit that, even during its worst days, it was always a staunch advocate of the need to provide a steady and reliable diet of official information, and was later to become a dedicated opponent of all forms of propaganda, successfully facing down demands from various quarters to spawn more of the wretched stuff. As early as August 1940, MoI had begun its gradual withdrawal from exhortation, reiterating the belief in its prime function to inform. Unfortunately, lack of information to release prevented MoI from living up to the maxim!

Indeed, it was the Service Ministries' early intransigence and unwillingness to release all but the blandest of bulletins which helped to reinforce the public impression that nothing at all was happening – the 'phoney war' syndrome. In March 1940, MoI had succeeded in forcing the Service Ministries to initial a draft agreement on news policy. MoI aspired to tell the truth and nothing but the truth and, as far as possible, the whole truth, while the Services 'undertook' to make MoI privy, and promptly, to all news and to delegate to it power to decide the form of news releases. Later writers were to confirm that MoI honoured the first part, but it is clear that they were often frustrated by the Services with regard to the second part. Even so, MoI's new doctrine began slowly to forge a new relationship between Government and people. In January 1941, it flatly refused to comply with pressure from the Service Ministries to mount a campaign intended to make the people more 'front-line minded', on the grounds that to do so would be useless and probably aggravating. That April, Bracken (not yet Minister) told the Cabinet 'there must be more explanation, not only about the armed forces but also about production, labour ... and the big problems that affect everyone today. We must stop appealing to the public, or lecturing to it. One makes it furious, the other resentful ... General appeals should not be made ... too many people are already working to the limit of their capacity or are unable to do so for reasons beyond their control'.

The role of HMSO is more simply explained. It was but an agency of Government, carrying out the tasks allotted to it. In theory, these were restricted to receiving the completed manuscripts from MoI, designing the format and appearance, arranging for the printing and distribution of each title, and assisting with the marketing and selling. In practice, though, its involvement was rather more creative, material and productive, and an impressive share of the credit, both for the series' initial success and permanent interest, properly belongs to HMSO.

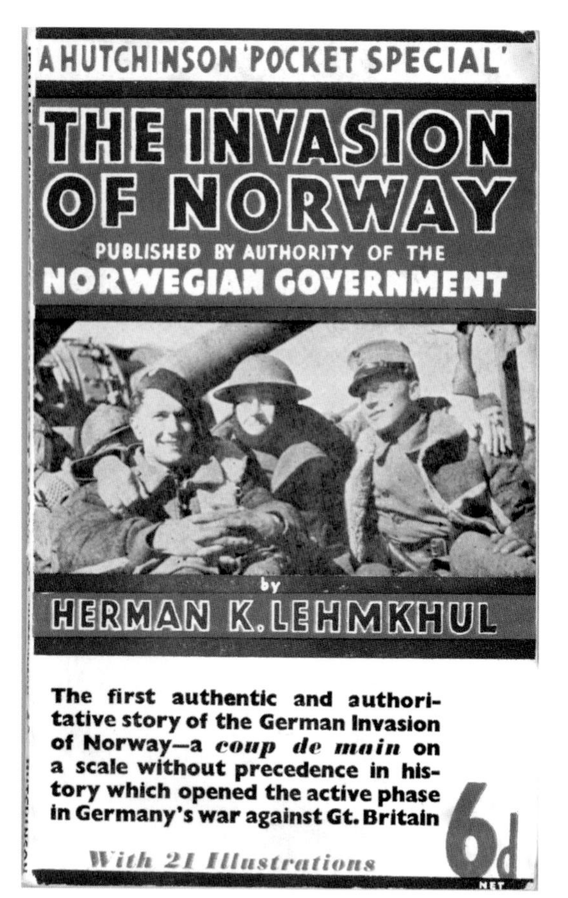

At the outset, MoI's policy (so far as it could then be complimented with having one) had been either to invite commercial publishers to prepare, with official help, manuscripts for publication, or to assist an author to do so and to find his own publisher; or even to prepare a manuscript, in-house, and offer it as a finished package to a commercial publisher. HMSO would thus have no involvement. Given the economic climate of the times, with its shortages of skilled labour and most materials – particularly of paper, the supply of which was closely controlled – and the incidence of distribution difficulties and, later, of bomb damage, the resulting publications were a pretty unimpressive lot.

They took various forms. Hutchinson, for example, put out a series of small, sewn paperbacks in light card covers: the Hutchinson 'Pocket Special' series, described as 'up-to-the-minute books on topics of moment written by eminent authorities', priced 6d. Withy Grove Press put out similar works under their Cherry Tree paperback imprint, and several mainstream hardback publishers also offered many cheaply-produced short books upon wartime subjects, in hard covers with dust wrappers, sold for a few shillings

each. Most were not illustrated; those that were, generally were not done well. There were also extensive crops of pamphlets-proper, relatively short, with wire-stitched pages in card covers, often sold for as little as 3d or 4d. Generally, all were produced in a rush, to take advantage of a passing opportunity, and today are hardly worth a passing glance – and most certainly not the prices often optimistically asked for them!

MoI's early reliance upon commercial publishing channels also included arrangements with (among others) Penguin Books, Oxford University Press, Hulton Press and Foyles' Book Clubs. Its ability to make paper available almost constituted an offer that no publisher could refuse. *Picture Post*, for example, published several MoI-agreed special-subject issues, while popular novelist Hugh Walpole was commissioned to write a small pamphlet which was distributed by Foyles with book club material sent to all members. Many of Penguin's special titles of that era are avidly collected to this day, despite their austere appearance and dated content, and now change hands at surprising prices.

But when MoI began to involve HMSO, the position changed dramatically, and substantially for the better. By that time, the Service Ministries were themselves directly commissioning manuscripts, usually from authors of stature and fame. These would be passed, via MoI, to HMSO, who would participate in the editing. There, studio work would mould the text to display the best features of modern book design. Good illustrations, often specially created for the pamphlet and with carefully prepared captions, would be melded with the story. Covers, with some early exceptions, would be expertly designed, often with the use of colour, sometimes with artwork prepared by leading artists. The resulting plates would be used to print on paper of higher quality than that usually available to commercial producers through their Ministry allocations.

Commercial publishers were, in any case, tempted to skimp on materials, perhaps to transfer saved Ministry paper, etc., to extend and embellish their more speculative titles.

The post-design work of printing and finishing would be allocated by HMSO to printers equipped to produce to a high standard, with the larger orders often shared amongst several printers around the country, and the finished, high-quality work put on sale at prices that must have made other publishers weep! Thus, in sharp contrast to their commercial competitors, HMSO provided the public and posterity with well-written, often superbly-produced mini-masterpieces at unrefusable prices. No wonder that the popularity of the series has endured for so long. Unhappily, many of these pamphlets are now approaching the limits of the physical endurance of their material parts, and are falling apart through the passage of time and much handling. Thereby, they are becoming harder to find and increasingly valued, especially those copies still in good condition. They have become a rapidly diminishing resource worthy of conservation, already difficult to access in reference collections.

It would be outside the scope of this book to deal at length with those MoI-inspired, but unacknowledged, titles that were published commercially without input from HMSO (though some are discussed in chapter 7) but, for purposes of comparison, some attention should be given here to those early MoI/HMSO (non-series) publications, the forerunners of the WW2 HMSO Paperbacks series that was to open so spectacularly in Spring 1941. At the outset, inevitably, these were restricted to pamphlets that either gave advice or attempted to influence opinion and morale. First to appear, and surprisingly early, was ***National Service*** which is internally dated January 1939 – that is to say, eight

Worse, the War Cabinet were anxious that aggressive attacks by the RAF should not provoke German reprisals that home defences could not repel, and they knew that it would not be possible to replace a high level of losses of bombers and their crews. As a consequence, at the beginning of the war, RAF bomber crews were restricted mainly to leaflet 'raids', reconnaissance, and attacks against German naval installations and shipping. For a while they were specifically prohibited from dropping their bombs on land!

These circumstances severely restricted Saunders' scope for compiling a narrative that could compare with the evident aggression of Fighter Command during the Battle of Britain and he was, of course, prevented from revealing the coming changes, for the first of the RAF's four-engined, long-range, heavy bombers were already in production and training in hand for their intended crews. What a wonderful boost that news would have given to the book and to its readers! Even so, it did well enough without it, and this second publishing triumph had important consequences.

Pilot and second pilot. Reprinted from **Bomber Command** ***(MoI/HMSO, 1941)***

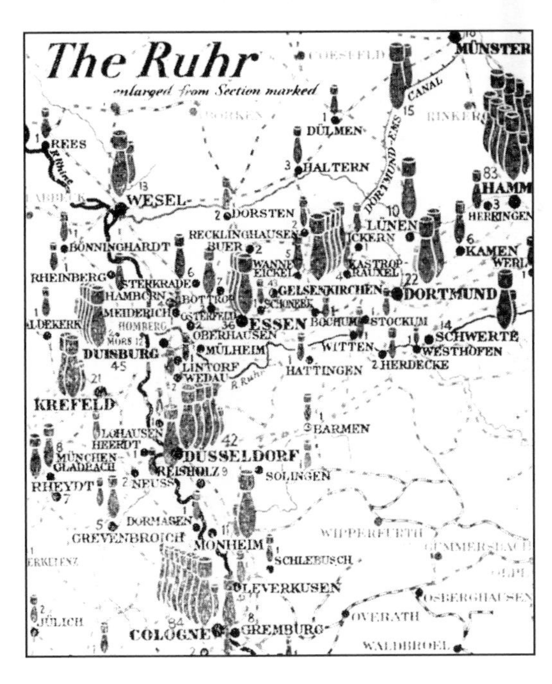

'Attack at the heart: the raids on Germany.' Reprinted from **Bomber Command** ***(MoI/HMSO, 1941)***

In his books of autobiography, H E Bates tells how, after earlier rebuffs from both MoI and RAF, in August 1941 he wrote to David

Garnett at the Air Ministry, and asked for special work. His application was timely, and he was invited for an interview at which he met Hilary Saunders and others. It was explained that it had been proposed to form a new section within RAF Public Relations, with the internal designation of PR II, to be headed by Saunders, part of whose brief would be to recruit creative writers to further the good work already established by *The Battle of Britain* and *Bomber Command.* Within two months, Bates had been commissioned into the RAF – probably the only person ever to have been recruited into a fighting service at war specifically to write short stories! Around the same time, Saunders also arranged the transfer of John Pudney, already in the RAF, whisking him literally from the midst of a senior Intelligence course. Both were to join Saunders' new section, and both would, in due course, add new titles to the MoI/HMSO Paperbacks series. Other famous names at Air Ministry Public Relations (though not in Saunders' PR II section) were R F Delderfield, Eric Partridge, Alan Melville, John Strachey and Philip Guedalla, as well as David Garnett, already mentioned.

Saunders now had to cope with the administration and forward planning of his section, but he did not allow that to cramp his creativity. His energy and his methods at PR II led to RAF Public Relations becoming ironically dubbed 'RAF Writer Command' and were to put the RAF well ahead at publicising their activities, outflanking the Army and leaving the taciturn Royal Navy figuratively dead in the water. His first two pamphlets, best-sellers both, helped to reinstate and consolidate the RAF's position in the public regard. Ironically these, his first solo writing efforts, far outsold the long list of all his jointly written 'Francis Beeding' and 'David Pilgrim' novels combined, and yet earned him nothing beyond his official salary. Indeed, he had to keep writing privately to pay his way and keep his family. Between 1940 and 1945, at least eight new books of his were commercially published in addition to his undiminished official output.

John Pudney has recorded that PR II was permanently in uproar, with Saunders returning from consultations with seniors, blazing sometimes with enthusiasm but more often with anger, entering the section like an angry lion released from circus duty. Along the passage outside was a low-slung ventilation duct and, when hyped-up, Saunders often forgot to duck, so that he seemed to Pudney to carry a permanent head-wound during those days.

Saunders quickly provided the RAF with three more successful pamphlets. First of these, somewhat of a pot-boiler in comparison with its predecessors perhaps, was the short but nonetheless interesting and well-written ***Air-Sea Rescue*** (MoI/HMSO 1942), which explained the organisation and operations of the air-sea rescue service in home waters. That was an area of RAF work very much in the public eye at the time. The dramas of the shot-up aircraft, trying but failing to make it home; the often wounded pilot's escape from the sinking plane into the cold sea; the high-speed rescue launches and the seaplanes anxiously searching before the onset of darkness, provided all the makings of a thrilling story. After the fall of France, the Germans operated their own rescue service, and there was often a race to gather one's own before he could be captured by the other side.

Next to come from Saunders was ***Bomber Command Continues*** (MoI/HMSO, 1942), a much shorter sequel to his earlier *Bomber Command*. Strangely, judging by the number of copies that have survived, this seems to have sold far less well, even though it has a somewhat more encouraging story to tell. Now he could begin to reveal what he had been obliged to omit from the earlier book. He extends the story to June 1942, by which time the heavy bombers were coming into service and Bomber Command was building towards its eventual massive strength. Also, it was no longer necessary to encourage the USA to join the war: their troops had already begun to arrive in Britain.

For the contemporary, well-blitzed reader at home, no doubt the high spot of this book was its graphic and detailed account of the first thousand bomber raid, launched on Cologne on 30 May 1942. There was no doubt that this raid was a success, both in what it achieved over the target, and by its effect upon morale at home and on future strategic policy for the RAF. What Saunders could not tell, reasonably enough, was that Bomber Command's frontline strength was little more than 400 aircraft at the time, and that the total strength of 1,047 aircraft assembled for the raid had been achieved by stripping the training and conversion squadrons, indenting upon the factories, and mustering just about any plane that could fly, including the unsuitable and incompetent.

Despite the loss of a record number of planes – forty-one – it was a remarkable performance and the percentage losses were considered acceptable in view of the raid's outcome. New tactics had been applied; a pathfinder force equipped with radio navigation aids had both found and marked the target for the following bombers; the whole force was concentrated in time and space so that the planes arrived in a continuous stream, saturating the defences and confining the raid to a mere ninety minutes duration. However, it proved impractical to continue raids at the same scale, and the 1,000 bomber force was used only twice more before it was dispersed. It had proven the point of the theoreticians, though, and the experience was to have a profound effect upon RAF future strategy. So far as MoI/HMSO's series was concerned, there was also to be an effect, to be touched upon in chapter 7. Here let it just be said that *Bomber Command Continues* ends with a statement that it was but an interim report. Unhappily, a final report in pamphlet form from HMSO, setting out the RAF's triumph over Germany, was never to appear.

A contemporary reviewer, in *John o' London's Weekly,* pointed a scornful finger at a paragraph of optimistic propaganda that had crept into Saunders' generally objective narrative. He objected to speculation upon the effect of bombing on German civilian morale, pointing out that British bombs might well have a similar effect to German ones: stiffening morale and reinforcing determination to support the military effort. It was a perceptive – if unpopular – point to make in October 1942 for, when Allied ground forces reached the devastated enemy cities a little over two years later, that was exactly what they found to have been the case. By then, the whole philosophy of strategic bombing was undergoing a radical re-think, and there were some in the High Command who feared that the verdict of history might be that a high proportion of Bomber Command's total of 57,143 dead had been condemned in an 'over-the-top' madness tragically reminiscent of WW1's 'lions led by donkeys'.

Though Saunders' pamphleteering was far from over, his departing publication for the Air Ministry was ***Coastal Command*** (MoI/HMSO, 1942), which also enjoyed a vast sale at home, and was translated into several other languages – including Afrikaans and Greek. It was another substantial sewn paperback, of 144 pages, and was one of the most expensive yet, at a heavyweight 2s – a lot to pay for a paperback in 1942. Its sales may well have been assisted by a tie-in with a cinema documentary film released at the same time, also titled *Coastal Command.* RAF Writer Command was getting good at these tie-ins, and had avoided being tarnished by the earlier ludicrous efforts of MoI, when the palpably absurd film *The Lion has Wings* was met in cinemas by an embarrassed silence, and was laughed at by the press.

The tasks of the aircrew of Coastal Command were to 'find the enemy, strike the enemy, protect our ships', and that was recognised by the public to be hard, lonely and dangerous work, carried out with great skill and dedication. As well as protecting seamen, killing the enemy and sinking his submarines, Coastal Command was helping to get ships through and so putting weapons into the Army's hands and food on everyone's table. There was a strong feeling that a large part of Bomber Command's efforts might well be transferred to similar work with greater effect on the war's outcome. Debate and interest among the public was keen at the time and, amongst many, has still not subsided.

All of these pamphlets, so far, had been anonymous and factual, but the next was to be different on both counts. ***One of Our Aircraft is Missing*** (Royal Netherland Government Information Bureau/ HMSO, 1942) was another film tie-in, and what we have now come to call 'faction', a fictional narrative based firmly upon an amalgam of factual experiences. It also bore its writer's name on its cover – Emeric Pressburger. In partnership with Michael Powell, Pressburger had founded The Archers film production company, and *One of Our Aircraft* was their first film. It was made with the full co-operation of the Air Ministry, the Admiralty and the War Office and had a powerful cast of popular actors. The film was highly praised by Winston Churchill, who believed that it delivered an important message in furtherance of the war effort.

Both the book and the film upon which it was based had to be fictional, for they dealt with a subject where the truth would have cost many lives and been counter-productive – resistance against the Nazis in occupied countries. It was an aspect of the war that was to be dealt with several times again in the series, factually as well as fictionally. This one told of the network of patriots who, at personal risk of torture and death, sheltered ditched aircrew and passed them

Reprinted from* One of Our Aircraft is Missing *(HMSO, 1942)

back to Britain. At home, people knew it was happening but, for the best of reasons, had little knowledge of how it was done, or realistic ideas of the appalling risks faced by resistance activists and their families. To emphasise the reality upon which this 'story' was based, the exiled Dutch Government included the grim factual details of the execution of five gallant Dutchmen in Summer 1941. There can be no doubt that *One of Our Aircraft*, story though it may be, deserves its place alongside the factual titles in the series.

As well as the mediums of print and film, broadcasting supported the war effort and many short radio talks by anonymous RAF personnel were heard on BBC radio. Selections of these were published commercially and also by MoI/HMSO as ***We Speak from the Air*** (1942) and ***Over to You*** (1943). These talks were extremely popular – over 280 were broadcast in 1941 alone, and a further 900 up to March 1943. The method was to invite RAF men and women with a tale to tell to write it in their own words. A radio producer would help them to refine and condense their manuscripts to the right length and the writer would then read it over the radio in a simple and direct, conversational style. The talks were given anonymously, and covered all aspects of service work and life, from the gallant to the mundane. Representative scripts were collected for publication; twenty-three in *We Speak from the Air* and a further thirty in *Over to You*. Both were small books, pocket-sized and without illustrations. They provide a compelling record of personal experiences, which help to bring alive the more formal pamphlet accounts of campaigns.

'Fl Lt Pudney (hatless) and Lt Col Solodovnik survey the devastation of Senglea, Malta, March 1943. Pudney was in Malta to write the official* The Air Battle of Malta *for the RAF.' Reprinted with permission from the Imperial War Museum

Hilary Saunders' work for Air Ministry was almost done (though two later contributions have still to be mentioned), and he was transferred to work in a similar capacity at Combined Operations HQ, where we shall meet him later.

PR II was disbanded, its work to be continued by a new section, PR 3, no longer directed by a mere seconded civilian but by Group Captain Leonard Dodds. Two of Saunders' recruits, though, were at work on important contributions to the series. One was John Pudney, whom we came across earlier, at Coastal Command, snatched from an intelligence course. In idle moments, Pudney wrote war poems and when he had enough to fill a small volume, Saunders asked Coastal Command's C-in-C, Sir Philip Joubert, to write a foreword. The warlike Joubert flatly refused, claiming he could write better poetry himself. A very cross Saunders then arranged for the book to be commercially published, even designing a book jacket for it. Another was H E Bates who, on arrival at PR II, was promptly sent off to Bomber Command with instructions to write the *Flying Officer X* short stories (later to appear in a paperback edition of 100,000 copies for Air Ministry, and commercially in hardback). As well as being important propaganda at the time, this book was later recognised to be one of the important

'Malta the target. Walled in to the north and south by enemy territory, and to the west by Vichy controlled Tunisia. Malta was isolated by nearly 1000 miles of sea from Gibraltar and over 800 from Alexandria, in 1941 the nearest Allied land bases.'
Reprinted from **The Air Battle of Malta** ***(MoI/HMSO, 1944)***

literary achievements of the war.

Pudney was assigned to write ***The Air Battle of Malta*** (MoI/HMSO, 1944), and set out in December 1942 by troopship to West Africa, thence by air across Africa to Khartoum, on to Cairo for briefing by Air Chief Marshal Tedder, and then across the Western Desert to sneak into beleaguered Malta under cover of darkness. Pudney was in Malta only for the final few weeks of its siege, but shared in the hunger and the danger, flew with the RAF, put to sea with the Navy, worked alongside the anti-aircraft crews, and was bombed and shot at while writing his manuscript. Such were the birth pangs of many of the titles in HMSO's WW2 Paperback series. Pudney recorded, some years later, that he flew back from Malta to hand in his finished work, to have no further contact with it until asked to make a few amendments. By the time it appeared in print, he had almost finished his next book for the series.

As he wrote later, these Air Ministry authors were given set subjects, paid only according to rank and remained anonymous. Full facilities were provided but (he claimed) there were no special privileges. However, he admitted that the actual writing could take place either at the Air Ministry or abroad, or even at home, depending upon the availability of material – which most airmen would probably regard as a privilege not to be scorned. The obtaining of material and the literary style were matters for individual enterprise: only the official deadline was strict.

Pudney's next assignment was to write ***Atlantic Bridge*** (MoI/HMSO, 1945) about RAF Transport Command, the building of the enormous base at sub-Arctic Newfoundland, and the hazardous ferrying of newly-built bombers straight from the factories of USA and Canada across the Atlantic. Only a few years before, Atlantic flights had been pioneering adventures, the stuff of headlines, and there was little experience and no infrastructure to support a regular

service. Indeed, initial help and training had to be provided by Canadian Pacific Railways and British Overseas Airways, until the RAF could spare the time and the men from their priority task of defending Britain.

Flights from Canada to Britain were of 3,467 miles direct to Prestwick, or 3,241 miles with a brief landing at Reykjavik, undertaken in bitter cold and foul weather, with little chance of rescue should the brand new planes, their paint scarcely yet dry, ditch in the icy Atlantic. Later, there were flights southwards through Brazil and then across the South Atlantic and the width of Africa to Cairo, through hurricane zones, across jungles, mountains and deserts. It was an epic adventure of the twentieth century. And yet, they were done and redone, time and again, under pressure, against the clock, and subject to attack. Pudney's own task, as mere recorder, was hazardous enough. He set out from London with only 10s in his pocket, to cross the Atlantic. The book was written partly in Montreal, partly in West Africa, and partly at home in Essex after having travelled 20,000 miles collecting his material and meeting his subjects.

H E Bates, meanwhile, had been sent to RAF Tangmere, a fighter station, to write ***There's Freedom in the Air*** (MoI/HMSO, 1944). There he met Czech and Polish pilots flying with the RAF, and fell under the spell of their bravery and skill. The book tells a stirring and ennobling story of the achievements of men who had escaped from their countries as they fell under Nazi occupation, to fight back in the air with matchless gallantry, not knowing the fates of their families at home, nor knowing whether they would ever be able to return to those homes again. Norwegians, Dutch, Belgians, French and Greeks also fought with the RAF, bringing honour to themselves and their native lands, and earning the unstinting admiration of their allies in arms.

Though there is no doubt that Bates wrote the book, he did not acknowledge it in his autobiographical writings, possibly feeling that he still had an obligation to remain anonymous. However, he did tell of writing two others, neither of which came to be published by HMSO. First of these was ***The Night Battle of Britain***, the story of the 1941 struggle to use night fighters to counter the Luftwaffe's bombers during the blitz, written at the request of Air Chief Marshal Portal. Though the manuscript was officially approved as a correct record, the needs of security were considered paramount at the time, and publication was at first postponed and finally abandoned. However, the manuscript was eventually rescued from the Public Record Office and hopes remain that it may still be published commercially.

The other was ***Flying Bombs Over England*** which met a similar fate because it told of an aspect of Germany's V-weapons campaign that had not then been released to the public at home, and there were official anxieties that a short HMSO pamphlet was not the place to break the news. By the time officialdom had made up its mind, the war was over and the opportunity lost. However, Bates' manuscript was eventually recovered from the Public Record Office, to be published by Froglets of Westerham in 1994, with modern illustrations. Although never appearing under HMSO's imprint, in view of its genesis it ought, surely, to be considered as part of the series.

From elsewhere in Air Ministry PR, Philip Guedalla was sent to the Middle East to write a book upon the new strategic concept and

unqualified success of RAF Middle East Command, an independent 'army of the air' that broke the moulds of air warfare history. Too big a subject for a pamphlet, it first appeared at full length as a commercial hardback, to be followed by the pamphlet, ***RAF Middle East*** (MoI/HMSO, 1945) that provided excerpts and dealt with later developments of this remarkable story. The Command was responsible for initiating air operations over an enormous area, for fighting a powerful enemy, and for co-operating with the battling Army and Navy from hundreds of airfields. It fought – and won – an air war the nature of which had never before been seen!

While the RAF had been so busy, there would have been every excuse for imagining that the commercial airlines had been mothballed for the duration. In fact, they had been fully extended throughout the war, and had accomplished some tasks which had been too big for a battle-committed RAF and far beyond the capabilities of its own very limited transport force. These included surveying, testing and establishing new long-range routes around the world, and particularly across its more remote and dangerous parts. It is easy for us today, used to trans-world flights in single hops of 6,000 miles or more, to forget that the large planes of the 1930s and 1940s needed to land every few hundred miles. That had been easy enough in pre-war Europe, but had become damnably difficult in war conditions, with the Mediterranean all but closed, and many countries in enemy hands or nervously neutral.

'In summer [the desert] was extremely hot and fly-plagued by day, but the cool of the evening was perfect.'
Reprinted from* RAF Middle East *(MoI/HMSO, 1945)

The mail run to Benghazi was now possible only to the heavy four-engined bombers based near Cairo. Halifaxes bombed by night, US Liberators by day. Ground Crews prepare a Halifax as the sun goes down.'
Reprinted from* RAF Middle East *(MoI/HMSO, 1945)

The RAF had too much on hand to spare the resources needed, and it fell to commercial airlines to plot long-haul routes and provide landing, lodging, re-fuelling and engineering facilities; to provide for the supply of spares; and to organise rescue and recovery plans. Commercially-operated flying boats were the only means of handling certain Government needs, and the only means of reaching Australasia when much of the Pacific was in Japanese hands. The story told in ***Merchant Airmen*** (MoI/HMSO, 1944) is an exciting and fascinating one, recounting an aspect of the war that had, undeservedly, largely escaped public notice.

The Air Ministry and the Admiralty collaborated with the story of the anti-submarine war, told by naval historian, 'Taffrail' (Capt Henry Taprell Dorling, RN) in ***Battle of the Atlantic*** (CoI/HMSO, 1946).

Though the RAF was fully involved, it is perhaps more fitting that the book should be dealt with in chapter 4. Hilary Saunders returned to the Air Ministry scene for their ***By Air to Battle*** (MoI/HMSO, 1945), the official account of the British First and Sixth Airborne Divisions, but this, too, is perhaps better dealt with in the next chapter, and is mentioned here only for the record, and as an excuse to sum up Saunders' contribution to the series. John Pudney wrote of how Saunders' ideas had caught on, with a brisk demand for the products of the Air Ministry team, and how the other Services and ministries were beginning to employ similar methods to proclaim their war achievements. Though his section was soon swallowed up in the machinery of a huge department, seen in retrospect it had been run with a good deal of fortuitous intelligence. Many square pegs had been put into square holes, assembling a talented collection of creative people.

When the war was over, Saunders returned to the House of Commons, where he became Librarian, reorganising the department and taking it successfully through a demanding period before retiring through poor health in 1950. Active to the end, he was privileged to collaborate in the writing of the official three-volume history, *Royal Air Force 1939–45 (HMSO, 1953-54)*, but which did not appear until after his death in 1951. Fittingly, this civilian is buried in an RAF cemetery, alongside the flying heroes he represented so well.

Though the war was over, RAF Writer Command remained in business, though much scaled down. Two important pamphlets that continued its wartime tradition were ***Berlin Airlift*** (CoI/HMSO, 1949) and ***A Future In It*** (CoI/HMSO, 1950), which gave a snapshot of RAF life in the new jet age. Both will be dealt with in chapter 8.

Chapter 3

War Office

The Army Turns Words into Weapons

The British Army did not share in the benefits enjoyed by the RAF during the run-up to WW2. Its planners and strategists were fully alive to the threats posed by the rise and march of Nazism, but their expenditure estimates had been cut to the bone by Parliament, and there were political restraints upon their activities; even those which could be carried out almost at no cost. Individual officers were deeply concerned about the disadvantages with which the Army seemed condemned to enter a new European war, and there were many instances of officers using their leave and travelling at their own expense to gather information and intelligence needed by their planning colleagues.

At the War Office, detailed plans covering foreseeable contingencies following the outbreak of a war had been compiled, and kept daily up to date – but these were plans for mobilising largely a paper force, armed with shopping lists for equipment still unordered for want of cash. True, there had been some modernisation. A degree of mechanisation had been put in hand, including the provision of under-armoured, under-gunned, infantry-style tanks. When put to the test these proved no match for German Panzers and their anti-tank weapons, even though some German regimental transport was still horse-drawn.

However, one warlike activity that the Government had allowed the Army to invest in was Public Relations, and a new Director of PR had been appointed as early as 1938. This was John Beith, better known as best-selling novelist and successful

playwright 'Ian Hay', a WW1 Territorial Major turned teacher who was persuaded to return to uniform with the rank of Major-General and a desk in Whitehall. That may well have seemed, in the anxious atmosphere of the Munich crisis, the Army equivalent of re-arranging the deck-chairs on the Titanic but Beith quickly proved an inspired choice, and did much excellent work.

Even while (and possibly before) Hilary Saunders at Air Ministry was at work on MoI/HMSO's *The Battle of Britain*, Beith was writing ***The Battle of Flanders*** (War Office/HMSO, 1941), apparently without prompting or input from MoI. This was a pocket-sized book of only sixty-four pages, illustrated only with a few maps, but it recounted a story that needed to be told, and it sold well. The earliest book to appear from the War Office, it seems intended from the outset to have been the first among others that would detail 'the army at war', a generic title that was to appear on at least another ten WW2 HMSO Paperbacks. Thus, the Army's thinking and action upon PR seems to have been early up-to-speed under Beith's guidance.

The need for this book was clear. The political commitment to come to France's aid, and the General Staff's advance planning, meant that within a week of the war's start the transportation was ready, and the British Expeditionary Force (BEF) began its move on September 10, to be greeted by advanced units already in France. It arrived on schedule and, thanks to secrecy and speed, without having been attacked en route. Though initially small, the force was quickly enlarged, relieving elements of the large, well-equipped French army for frontier defence. What was to follow was a heroic tragedy, for BEF's fate was sealed almost from the start of the campaign. The attitude of the French Government was peculiar and unhelpful, their months before MoI was able to emerge from the shadows and admit to its existence. Perhaps for that reason, HMSO was given the sole credit for being the publisher. The book gives the lie to the widely-believed myth that Britain went into war totally unprepared. In fact, preparations of a sort had been in hand since 1934, little over a year after the Nazi Party came to power and Hitler was appointed Chancellor.

National Service (HMSO, 1939) is subtitled 'a guide to the ways in which the people of this country may give service', and its forty-eight pages are packed with basic information upon an amazing array of organisations clearly already in place for offensive, defensive and support activities. The pamphlet bears no price, for it was distributed free to every household in the country (it is still relatively easy to find, today), and included two 'post paid' enrolment application forms. Profiting from the lesson learned in 1914–18 that it was unwise to allow patriotic fervour to proceed unchanneled, it was designed to prevent impulsive and misdirected volunteering – the scramble by talented square pegs to find the nearest round hole in which to waste their energies. Instead, it offered suggestions to many civilian trades as to appropriate ways to serve the country by making use of present skills, as well as in more martial ways. Advice was provided for both men and women, across the age groups, in a range of full-time and part-time pursuits. It would be almost impossible for those taking the trouble to read the book to claim that their services were not wanted, or that they had nothing useful to offer. It is an impressive first attempt! By mid-summer (i.e. before war began) there had been 300,000 volunteers for the armed forces and 1.5 million recruits for the civil defence services.

Call to National Service

FROM THE PRIME MINISTER

10, Downing Street,
Whitehall,

January, 1939.

The desire of all of us is to live at peace with our neighbours. But to ensure peace we must be strong. The Country needs your service and you are anxious to play your part. This Guide will point the way. I ask you to read it carefully and to decide how you can best help.

Neville Chamberlain.

Reprinted from National Service (HMSO, 1939)

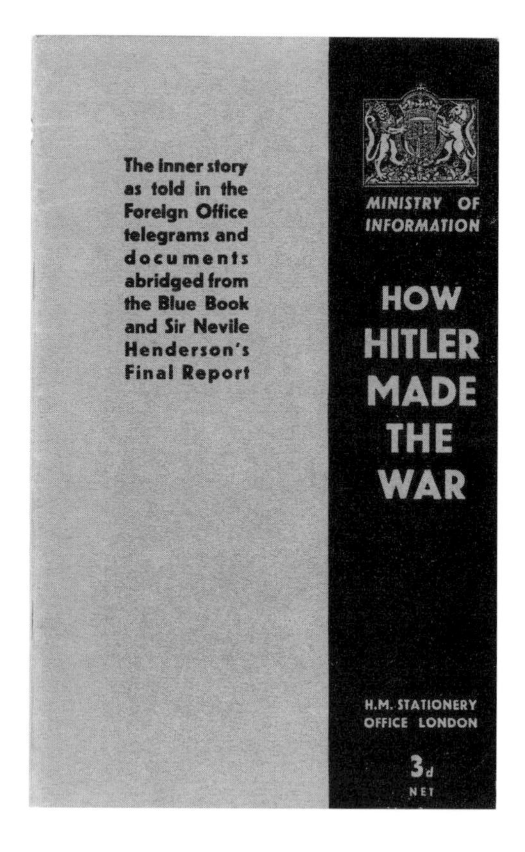

Almost immediately upon the declaration of war, the Government published as a Blue Book its official report disclosing the diplomatic exchanges concerning German–Polish relations and the outbreak of hostilities between Great Britain and Germany and a shorter publication giving Sir Neville Henderson's Final Report on the circumstances leading to the termination of his mission to Berlin. These two works were expertly condensed into a pamphlet, ***How Hitler Made The War*** (MoI/HMSO, 1939). One of the earliest publications to carry the MoI imprint, it sold for only 3d. Its forty-four pages provide a masterly summary of the steps set out in detail in the two longer books, and could have left none of its readers in doubt about Nazi provocation to manoeuvre Poland into a war, nor of Britain's mission to prevent an escalation to world conflict. As a 'first draft of history', the pamphlet might seem to have strong claims for inclusion within the WW2 HMSO Paperbacks series – except that it does not deal at all with the war, but only with attempts to avoid it.

Markedly different was ***The Assurance of Victory*** (MoI/HMSO, 1939), which appeared at Christmas time. Its five sections (why we are at war; how the world lines up; the fighting forces; sinews of war; the home front) dress up and support its central message: Chamberlain's propaganda-type statement that 'the allies are bound to win in the end, and the only question is how long it will take them to achieve their purpose'.

Though undoubtedly true as far as it went – and even privately acknowledged by Hitler – it was nonetheless propaganda, for it was designed to influence opinion and stiffen morale by telling less than 'the whole truth and nothing but the truth'. Compounded by the rather half-hearted attitude of the French government, obvious from the outset, Britain's first task was, surely, not to hold on for long enough to win in the end but, because of its relative military unpreparedness, to avoid defeat in the short-run by a well-prepared enemy with a record of successful short, sharp and decisive pre-emptive strikes. The British Government had already announced that it was planning for a war that would last three years ('the immense staying power of democracy is the first guarantee of Allied triumph'), but Hitler knew that he must lose such a long war, and intended to rely upon his unorthodox methods to avoid defeat.

The pamphlet did, though, make the wholly legitimate point that Britain had striven to ameliorate the harsher provisions of the Treaty of Versailles, whose post-WW1 sanctions against Germany had been one of the prime causes of the internal German problems and frustrations that had led, indirectly, to the rise to power of Hitler and the Nazi Party. Even after Hitler became Chancellor, the pamphlet pointed out, Britain continued every effort to integrate Germany into a peaceful Europe but the German government, misled by their leader, inflicted a treacherous foreign policy upon their neighbours. Britain had thus been left with no alternative but to try to prevent Germany from trampling upon the rights of other nations. That, after all, had long been Britain's consistent policy in the face of attempts by any Power to dominate Europe by force, and its continuation into the present day was entirely predictable.

1940 saw the publication of another type of pamphlet, worthy of mention here although also inappropriate for inclusion within the WW2 HMSO Paperback series. That was ***The Battle of the River Plate*** (HMSO, 1940). In external appearance, it resembled a Parliamentary White Paper (although it was no such thing) or, perhaps, one of the series of supplements to the *London Gazette* that were to be brought out from time to time to inform the people upon military or naval encounters of special significance, thus continuing a long tradition of such Government publications. It was an account of the events before, during and after the naval engagement, up to the scuttling of the German pocket-battleship – *The Admiral Graf Spee* – compiled in the Admiralty from the dispatches of Rear-Admiral Harwood and the Captains of HMSS *Ajax*, *Achilles* and *Exeter*. It was thus not a specially written contemporary account of the pursuit and battle (a 'first draft of history') but, rather, a compilation from the actual reports of the commanders to their directing authorities. There were to be many similar publications during the next few years and, to be consistent, the first of them should be regarded as outside the series, just as are all the subsequent examples.

It is important to remember that what has come to be thought of as the WW2 HMSO Paperbacks series was not, in fact, conceived as a potential series at all, and it seems highly unlikely, even when new titles were being prepared, that any of those were seen as providing further links for an already existing chain. The label 'series' is one which has been attached only many years later, and then mainly to separate and distinguish those MoI/HMSO pamphlets that provided a contemporary view of wartime history from those which did no such thing and were published for entirely different reasons.

In that context, the term 'series' has a meaning entirely different from its more usual application in the publishing glossary. Ordinarily, if a publisher used the term 'series' it would imply similarities of format and appearance, and an orderly progression through a subject; a sequence of volumes that would build to a complete set. The MoI/HMSO 'series' is no such thing, and its publishers did not use the term. No attempt was ever made to seek uniformity of size or appearance, and subjects were chosen fortuitously as opportunities arose. No doctrine of progression or infilling was ever applied, there are notable gaps, and there could never be any question of a search for completeness. Inputs to the series came from a variety of sources, some of which were clearly less willing to contribute than others – the Admiralty, indeed, had to be dragged, protesting to the end its objections, into the publisher's office!

It is not surprising, therefore, that it took a long time for anything resembling an editorial philosophy to develop; there was certainly no sign of one in 1939 and 1940. Government and Cabinet were each in two minds about what should be the nature of official publicity while, at that time, MoI had yet to discover any mind of its own to make up! Chamberlain's Government had believed that the people should be kept informed, but as yet had little confidence in the nation's ability to absorb bad news and maintain its morale. The Cabinet initially felt that instruction and propaganda should form the front line of official publicity, and it was to be several years before a revitalised MoI, under Brendan Bracken, would be able to convince the Cabinet that the safest and surest way to bolster and support morale was to keep the people fully and promptly informed of the bad news as well as the good. Slowly they came to see that honesty and explanation were far more effective than campaigns insulting to the intelligence and courage of even the faint-hearted. Eventually, Bracken's MoI became strong and confident enough to insist upon Governmental recognition of the intelligence and resolve of the public, and it finally persuaded the nation's leaders that victory itself depended upon a frank and open acknowledgement of partnership between people and Government. Though much of the morale-sustaining effect of knowing what was going on was due to the nature and cultural personality of the British people, in the fullness of time even Dr Goebbels came to realise its power and to advocate adoption of the principle in Germany.

It took several silly and serious mistakes before that lesson was properly understood. The earlier period of phoney war, from September 1939 until the German assaults on Holland and Belgium, and breakthrough into France in May 1940, had done nothing to help to develop an understanding of what would be required for effective official publicity. During that time, with little to report (or, perhaps more accurately, little reported), there were almost no issues upon which the publicists could practise their techniques and learn their trade. People at home, perhaps sensing a lack of trust, became disillusioned with their leaders, bored with the non-war that was disrupting their lives and ambitions seemingly for no purpose, and their interest and attention had begun to wander. In terms of morale, it had been a dangerous moment.

When serious fighting began, the news it generated was almost unrelievedly bad. The public resented the Service Ministries' reluctance to release any news at all, combined with censorship policies seemingly designed to guarantee that any news which did escape would be seriously delayed and probably misleadingly out of date. Public dissatisfaction was made obvious by the huge numbers who felt the need to listen regularly to the enemy's news and propaganda broadcasts from Radio Hamburg. In the absence of the home-grown variety, foreign news reports – and even quotes from Lord Haw-Haw – were given prominence in British newspapers, much to the annoyance of the Service Ministries, who often found themselves seriously embarrassed by what was printed and openly discussed wherever people met. The Government found it necessary to mount a campaign to discourage the spreading of rumours – rumours caused by its own lack of attention to the legitimate needs of the public for official news.

During all this turmoil, MoI was of no use to the Government that had misbegotten it, nor to the media which looked to it for assistance, nor to the people who relied upon it for news. It was caught up in its own problems. Its own Parliamentary Secretary said of it that his Ministry was staffed with duds at the top, with all the good people in the most subordinate positions, while *The Observer* had written of 'the stupefying absurdity with which it had been staffed'. Its initial lack of any properly defined mission, and lack of delegated powers to enforce its authority upon the Services' PR departments was compounded by a series of staff-shedding contractions; compensatory expansions; reorganisations of structure; relinquishing of some areas of responsibility and the gathering of others. Occasionally today's decision would be reversed tomorrow, and then reinstated next week. Prevented from directing activities, it turned inwards and became obsessed with structure and organisation, and came close to ignominious dissolution.

One frustrated senior official had even gone so far as to ask the King to intervene – and had received his promise of help. No wonder that the radio comedian Tommy Handley publicly caricatured it as 'the Ministry of Aggravation'! Widely condemned as being wasteful and over-staffed when its staff numbers had been reduced to well under one thousand, significantly it was later to escape criticism when, in 1943, its staff was revealed to be three times that number. A measure, perhaps, of the extent to which it had, by then, cleaned up its image and reputation?

MoI's first Minister, Lord MacMillan, wrote afterwards that he had never understood why he had been taken from the Bench to run the new department of state, and he resigned as soon his replacement had been found, after only four months in office. He was followed by Sir John Reith (of BBC fame) who had at first flatly refused the office until persuaded that it was his patriotic duty to accept it. Reith also remained at MoI for just four months, before handing over to Duff Cooper who made no secret of his lack of enthusiasm for the job and of his desire to quit it as soon as he decently could. Reith was later to write about the unhappy muddle of his time at MoI: 'What would Dr Goebbels have thought of it all?

... How he would have laughed if he could have believed a tenth of what was happening!' But let's restore some perspective here. It seems safe to surmise that Dr Goebbels would probably have commented, 'You lucky man. I had my own troubles, too, you know. At least you could resign and walk away from yours.' The only way that Goebbels could extricate himself was first to 'resign' his wife and young family by killing them, and then to 'resign' himself by the same route. As Winston Churchill famously said, 'democracy is the worst system there is, except for all the others that have been tried.'

In time, an official report upon the effectiveness of Governmental machinery was to compliment Bracken's MoI with the words 'thoroughness and solidity, combined with flexibility and enterprise, the hallmarks of administrative efficiency'. It had come triumphantly through its early troubles, to be acknowledged as a success, both with censorship and anti-censorship, and had learned to rebuff the many pressures that might have turned it into merely an instrument of suppression. Before this transformation, MoI had also got through two Parliamentary Secretaries, two executive heads, and countless department chiefs. Churchill had finally lost patience with the whole silly pantomime, and appointed his pal and, more relevantly, successful press proprietor with a go-getting reputation, Brendan Bracken, as Minister; no doubt with a brief to knock a few heads together and restore order and purpose. This he did, in double-quick time, and with his team of Ernest Thurtle as Parliamentary Secretary and Cyril Radcliffe (recruited to MoI from the Bar, and later to become Lord Radcliffe) as Director General, they were to remain there until the Ministry began to wind down. In 1945, Bracken asked Churchill if he could dissolve MoI, but was instructed to keep it in existence at least until the defeat of Japan, though on a reduced scale. Bracken himself was allowed to go upon the surrender of Germany. MoI lingered on until March 1946, when its remaining functions were laid elsewhere. So far as Government publicity was concerned, responsibility came to be vested in a new Central Office of Information (still in business in the 1990s), who were to publish the final, post-war titles in the WW2 HMSO Paperbacks series.

Bracken's team at MoI were to benefit from the gradual, but useful, change of attitude towards public relations within the Service Ministries, and it was from 1941 that MoI's earlier policy of making use of commercial publishers and freelance authors underwent its fundamental change. Almost certainly those changes had begun before Bracken's appointment, but it was his administration that was to extend their reach and reap the benefit of them. From 1941, pamphlets were to be commissioned by the several sponsoring ministries – mostly the Service Ministries, but also by the Ministries of War Transport, Home Security, Health, Labour and National Service, Aircraft Production, Supply, the Board of Education, the Colonial Office – even by some Service Commands and Allied Governments. Others were directly sponsored by MoI itself, while HMSO occasionally acted directly for sponsoring departments without any obvious MoI involvement. It was a much more flexible – and effective – system, and both the authority and the quality of output were transformed.

At least part of the credit must be given to two well-known authors who had arrived in positions of influence, one at the Air Ministry, the other at the War Office. A third, though less influentially placed at MoI, at least had a direct line to the Admiralty via the 'old boy network'. Later chapters will provide the details but it is right to introduce the reader to the initiators of this change of fortune: John Beith (better known as author 'Ian Hay') at the War Office and Hilary Saunders ('Francis Beeding') at the Air Ministry. They were to provide some of the best of the pamphlets themselves, and to recruit and inspire others to follow in their footsteps. The third was Henry Taprell Dorling (the author, 'Taffrail'), a retired Captain RN, who was brought out of retirement to stiffen the naval liaison section at MoI, and who was eventually able to ensure that the Royal Navy (though still against its better judgement) began at last to share the limelight until then

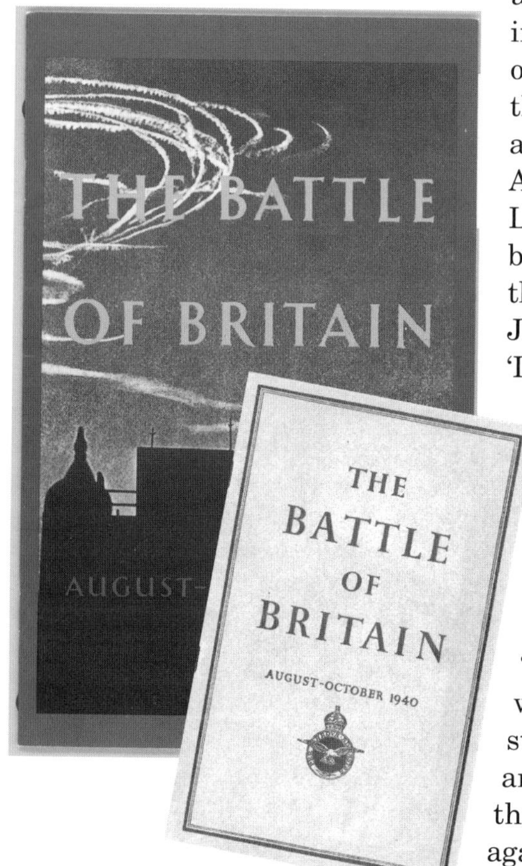

exclusively enjoyed by the Royal Air Force and the Army. Their writers' understanding of the stories that needed to be told, and of the need for top-flight authors to tell them, is responsible for the high standard of the stream of pamphlets that were to appear under HMSO's imprint throughout the rest of the war and into the early post-war period.

The new regime had two immediate best-sellers, ***The Battle of Britain*** and ***Bomber Command*** (both MoI/HMSO, 1941 – see next chapter), as well as other, lesser, triumphs appearing in 1941 and 1942. The Government and MoI were insistent that civilians should regard themselves as also serving in a front line; the Blitz and the Baedeker raids, as well as conscription for war work at home, reinforced that. Soon the Home Front, too, would be provided with a record of its determined support of the fighting forces.

It is from such a starting position that our story begins in earnest.

Chapter 2

Air Ministry

RAF Writer Command

While MoI was conducting its private war within its 'ivory tower', the rest of Britain had been going through an exciting time of its own. Probably nowhere was that more strikingly evident than at the Air Ministry, where the myth that Britain had entered WW2 totally unprepared must have brought wry smiles to the faces of RAF planners and strategists.

The RAF had enjoyed an advantage over the Army and Royal Navy because it had been required to maintain an active service role in the Middle East between the wars, particularly in Iraq where, since October 1922, it had carried full responsibility for both defence and security. That policy, adopted for reasons of economy in manpower and defence costs as well as for sound military reasons, had provided RAF staff, ground- and air-crews with extensive target-finding, attack and rescue experience in circumstances largely denied to their colleagues in the other Services. Then, from 1934, the perceived need to counter the new dangers posed by the build-up of Nazi Germany's Luftwaffe gave a special impetus to the RAF campaign for expansion and re-equipment.

Between 1934 and the Spring of 1939, the RAF had been expanded from a force of some 30,000 regulars and 11,000 reservists to nearly 120,000 regulars and 70,000 reservists. First line aircraft based in Britain had increased from 564 mostly wooden bi-planes with fixed undercarriages, constant-pitch airscrews and open cockpits to 1,500 aircraft, many of them all-metal monoplanes with retractable undercarriages, variable pitch airscrews and high performance engines. The best-performing fighter of 1934, the Fury 2, had a top speed of 220 mph and a ceiling of 20,000 ft. The 1939 Hurricane Mk 1 could climb to over 30,000 ft and fly at over 300 mph, while the Spitfire Mk 1 flew at 350 mph, and had an operating height of 33,000 ft. The Fury's two .303 Vickers WW1 machine guns had been superseded by the Hurricanes' and Spitfires' eight Browning .303 guns, with greater reliability and a higher rate of fire.

Although there is no doubt that Britain entered the war with serious performance deficiencies in its bomber types, their speeds, carrying capacities and radiuses of action had increased. For example, the 1934 Heyford would have had difficulty in flying a war mission from England to Paris and back, whereas the 1939 Wellingtons could – and did – reach Hamburg with greater bomb-loads, and return. Unhappily, those hardware improvements had not yet been matched by comparable advances in night navigation and target finding, shortcomings which were destined seriously to cramp Bomber Command's style throughout the first three years of war. Fighter Command, though, already enjoyed the inestimable benefit of the home defence radar installation almost from the outset.

Though the public did not know all of this at the time, they knew enough to invest the RAF with a special glamour, and to be thirsty for knowledge and news of its flyers and their planes. A mystique about the RAF had developed in the eyes of the nation, reinforced during the early months of the war when it seemed – wrongly – to be the only arm of the Services actually in contact with the enemy, and later by its visible and clearly vital struggle with the Luftwaffe during the Battle of Britain. Though the nation was both fond and proud of its Army and Navy, it did not afford them equivalent interest and emotional support, which gave rise to some inter-services friction, and was also to influence the early history of MoI/HMSO pamphlets.

However, the RAF received an unjustifiably bad press during the collapse of France and the Dunkirk evacuation, and the Air Ministry resolved to redress the situation with a PR campaign. The Minister of Information acknowledged, with gratitude, that the RAF was the most co-operative of the Services – they did, after all, have most with which to co-operate. The Battle of Britain was to provide the ideal vehicle, and the RAF became the first of the Services to abandon the 'sealed lips' policy. Much of the credit for the way in which that was done, and for its amazing success, must be given to that key figure in HMSO's series, Hilary Saunders.

Hilary Aiden St George Saunders had entered the Welsh Guards as a ranker, straight from school in 1916, was soon commissioned, and won a Military Cross for 'conspicuous gallantry and devotion to duty' on the Western Front. After service in Belgium and France, at the war's end he went up to Oxford to study history, but was soon diverted to more immediately useful matters, thanks to a vacation job helping with the removal of the new League of Nations from London to Geneva. Instead of returning to complete his studies, he joined the League's Secretariat, and worked as an international civil servant until, on the death of his wife, and disillusioned by the League's evident failure to control Hitler's aspirations for Germany, he returned to London in 1937. During that period, he had achieved fame (though not riches) mainly in partnership with his friend and colleague at the League, John Palmer, as a writer of thrillers and historical novels, under their joint-pseudonyms of 'Francis Beeding' and 'David Pilgrim'.

In 1938, Saunders joined the staff of the House of Commons but, on the outbreak of war, immediately offered his services to the war effort. Still as a civilian (he was now in his 40s), he was promptly seconded to the Admiralty but, very soon, as an accomplished linguist, was transferred to liaison officer at France's Ministry of Information, and had an exciting, last-minute escape as the Germans reached Paris. The 'Francis Beeding' novel, *Eleven Were Brave* (Hodder & Stoughton, 1940) provides a fascinating insight into the atmosphere and circumstances of that perilous time, written by one who was there.

On Saunders' return to England, he was again transferred, this time to Air Ministry, where he was later to succeed in creating a special section for himself in its PR department. There he would go on to pluck creative writers from their Service postings and both drive and inspire them to follow his lead as a provider of some of the very best of MoI/HMSO WW2 pamphlets.

His first task was to write the definitive contemporary record, ***The Battle of Britain*** (MoI/HMSO, 1941), which sold 300,000 copies on the first day of its appearance in March 1941. This first version was without illustrations, a modest-seeming thirty-two page pamphlet in a light card, air force blue wrapper, price 3d. The demand for this somewhat dull-looking document seemed inexhaustible, and further impressions were rushed out while HMSO quickly redesigned and repackaged it into a more exciting looking, eye-catching, larger, thirty-six page pamphlet with a wrap-around artwork-enhanced paper cover, plus action photographs and diagrams. Despite its price increase to 6d, its sales ran to millions, with copies being printed and rushed around the world, in many languages.

There is no record of how many copies were printed and sold – one estimate is as high as 15 million copies. Certainly HMSO's own printers had delivered 2 million copies by 1945 and the text had been extensively printed elsewhere under licence, both in Britain and around the world. The pamphlet was again in print, in an HMSO edition, in 1989 and its text also recently appeared as an appendix within an eye-witness account of life in wartime London. The quoted estimate of 15 million copies may be a little optimistic, but is nonetheless a reasonable guess. For example, Hilary Saunders' MoI text had been abridged and adapted by David Garnett for Penguin Books, who published it in their Puffin Picture Book series, both in Britain and USA, while the full text was also published in USA by Doubleday, Doran & Co, both in 1941. American sales were vast, hyped by a Hollywood-style promotional campaign for the books, and a more subtle propaganda effort to interest that country in the struggle against Nazism and to persuade it to join in.

Saunders was later to explain how he compiled his material and wrote his texts, and it is clear that he had been provided with a free hand to travel and interview the participants, and to examine the combat records and intelligence reports in detail. With hindsight, and the benefit of much post-war research, including analysis of Luftwaffe records (denied, of course, to Saunders), we now know that Saunders' text contains some inaccuracies, and that it repeats some of the optimistic official 'statistics' extrapolated from the combat reports taken by RAF Intelligence Officers from pilots immediately after landing. Even so, the book manifestly is exactly what it was purported to be – a 'first draft of history', compiled from evidence given before the guns had cooled, before the bleeding had stopped.

Saunders and others have left a record of the techniques used by MoI's writers. Each pamphlet had to be built upon two solid foundations: official records not otherwise available, and personal stories collected firsthand from the combatants. Before Saunders wrote this text, he consulted secret operational plans; force commanders' reports and conclusions; the daily situation reports compiled throughout the eighty-four days the battle lasted; Squadron and Flight diaries; and over a thousand individual combat reports scribbled in haste by the pilots after each sortie. Some years later, Saunders wrote that no Government pamphlet he had read or written had told the whole truth, but not one of them had contained a lie. The reader had not been told everything, but neither had he been told what was not believed true. None of the MoI pamphlets had, in Saunders' opinion, ever yielded to the temptation to deceive. His own orders, he made clear, had always been to write the truth as he had seen it and had been able to discover it. On occasions, some of his words were removed on official orders, but never were any added that he had not himself written.

Saunders stated clearly that the pamphleteer's job was to write contemporary history, not to weigh everything judicially and search every source like an historian. He must be content with less. He knew that combat reports by tired, often injured men sometimes contradicted each other, and that two men under stress sometimes saw a single incident differently. The reader must allow for that, just as he did when reading his daily paper or listening to the radio news. That same reader must also observe carefully what is written and what is omitted. Saunders gave as an example the statement in *The Battle of Britain* that the RAF's squadrons were stronger at the end of the battle than they had been at the beginning. That was literally true, but what was not said was that there were fewer pilots, nor that, in the later stages, the RAF had been unable to replace the casualties it had suffered. Clearly, it would have been wrong to reveal in 1941 to a still unbeaten enemy that there had been a shortage of pilots. However, that fact would be told by 1944. Later knowledge has thrown a new light upon what was believed at the time, but the intended truth, virtual completeness and substantial accuracy of MoI/HMSO's *The Battle of Britain* pamphlet published in March 1941 are nonetheless still to be triumphantly proclaimed.

As a result of the runaway success of his first pamphlet, Saunders was immediately instructed to do for Bomber Command what he had so effectively done for Fighter Command. By May 1941, he was visiting bomber stations, collecting his material and

interviewing the returning aircrews. He worked quickly, compiling a record of operations from September 1939 to July 1941, and his next pamphlet, a substantial sewn paperback of 128 pages, ***Bomber Command*** (MoI/HMSO, 1941), was on sale by early Autumn in a coloured cover with a wraparound reproduction of a dramatic painting by Nockold. It was to prove another blockbusting best-seller for MoI, despite its much higher price of 1s 6d. Sales were no doubt helped by its arrival in bookshops around the time the dramatic film documentary, *Target for Tonight*, reached local cinemas after its release in July 1941.

So high was the demand for copies that production by the severely restricted home printing industry had to be shared among many printers around the country. Not all of those had retained the capability to reproduce Nockold's cover painting in colour, so that a monochrome photographic alternative had to be provided by some of them. The book was also printed abroad, in other covers, including large editions in USA and Canada. The American edition, from Doubleday, Doran & Co, was again treated to Hollywood-style hype in the bookshops, coupled with a softly-softly approach on the lecture circuit and public platforms. Battle-scarred, much-decorated bomber captains were sent around USA to talk of their experiences and encourage support from concerned Americans, so that a discreet pressure was maintained upon the US Government to join the fight against Nazism.

With our later knowledge of their triumphs and heroism, it is difficult not to feel sorry for the personnel of Bomber Command at that low point in their fortunes. At the outbreak of war, the squadrons were provided with slow, low-capacity, short-range planes that could barely defend themselves, while their crews, though well-trained in other aspects, had poor-quality target-finding aids and indifferent bomb-sights. They were thus hard put to deliver the blows to the enemy that their spirit and professional ability enabled.

political will to resist doubtful, and many French troops were demoralised and resentful. The German breakthrough came many miles from the British lines, and the BEF quickly found itself outflanked and unsupported.

Their enforced retreat across Flanders towards Dunkirk was well conducted and fought with gallantry and honour, and a splendid diversionary stand at Calais was to form the subject of another book in the series. Evacuating an army across open beaches, without port facilities, inevitably meant that all heavy equipment had to be abandoned, but 337,000 trained and experienced men were rescued and returned to Britain – including over 100,000 French troops. A 'forlorn hope' contingent was purposely left behind at Calais to divert and delay the Germans while British soldiers in Central France continued to fight on. The British had been pushed out rather than defeated, seemingly as much by their ally as by their enemy. They had lost most of their weapons and transport, and were physically exhausted, but their honour was intact. Good leadership was soon to restore their fighting spirit, and contemporary publications were full of references to their keenness to get back into battle.

Beith had recruited the successful novelist, Eric Linklater (of whom more in a moment) into Army PR, and he provided both a companion booklet and a sequel. First came his ***The Defence of Calais*** (MoI/HMSO, 1941), a real-life '*Boys Own* blood-and-thunder' episode of gallantry and self-sacrifice worthy of the best of British Army traditions. The General Staff's view was that any hope for the recovery of heavy weapons and transport was unrealistic without extensive port facilities and more time than the Germans would allow, but the Germans would expect them to try. Therefore, deceive the enemy into believing that Calais docks were essential and draw them into full-scale efforts to capture the town and so deny use of its port installation. Behind this cunning smokescreen, the main army could be spirited away with minimised risk. It was a daring plan, and it needed heroes to carry it through. The defenders of Calais were not asked to volunteer, but they bravely accepted the challenge, and fought hard, for the benefit of their escaping comrades.

Linklater wrote his text in the form of a day-by-day record but, although he interviewed a number of the participants and had full access to official records, he had to confess that his could be only

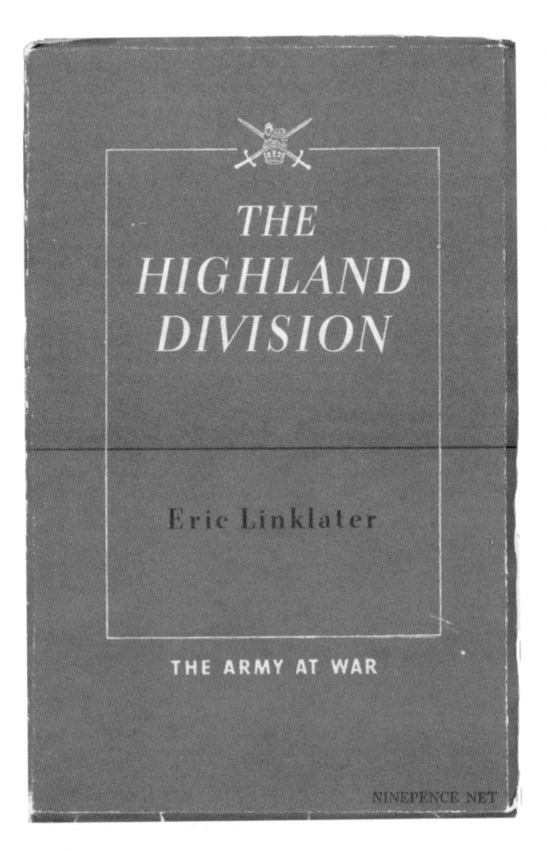

an interim report, for much had been enacted by little groups of men who, with no witnesses but their enemy, had fought until killed. Most of the survivors had been taken into what promised to be a long captivity. But several of those had quickly escaped and found their way back to Britain, to contribute to this record. Linklater called it, 'a half-told tale: of such a story even a fragment is worth the telling'.

Though the Army in Flanders had escaped to Britain, other elements of the BEF continued fighting in the Allied retreat from the Maginot Line and, far from considering France to be already lost, additional troops were sent from Britain to join them even while the Dunkirk evacuation was being planned. Linklater's sequel pamphlet was ***The Highland Division*** (MoI/HMSO, 1942), which concentrates upon the epic story of the 51st Division. Because of a shortage of news, the surrender of two of its brigades in June 1940 gave rise to feelings of shock, even of shame, at home. It soon emerged, though, that the 51st had upheld and enhanced its proud record in that sternest test of discipline, a long rearguard action. It suffered many casualties, but maintained to the last a fine aggressive spirit and stubbornness in defence. It had become trapped in a rout of French troops, and so outflanked and surrounded. The Division had become a byword for high morale and fighting spirit, so that French soldiers who had earlier fought alongside had found those qualities to be contagious. Indeed, General de Gaulle, seldom guilty of a good word about his allies, openly declared that it was that very spirit of the 51st which determined him to continue fighting to the end, no matter what might be the course of events. Their German captors did not find it easy to keep soldiers of the 51st in the bag, and several were to escape back to Britain – including one from as far away as Poland, who travelled home via Bulgaria in time to be interviewed for Linklater's book.

To avoid confusion, *The Defence of Calais* and *The Highland Division* have been dealt with out of sequence, so that it is now necessary to return to the Summer of 1939. Eric Linklater had long been living in Orkney, and was on the list of Reserve Officers for the Territorials. The surrounding area was to be turned into an extensive 'open fortress' to better protect the naval ships and installations at Scapa Flow. He was invited to enrol, to command a mainly locally-raised contingent of Royal Engineers who would construct AA and coastal defences throughout the area. Because his duties involved much local travel between the islands, and because of his skills as a writer, about January 1941 the War Office asked him also to visit the other island groups and Iceland, to write ***The Northern Garrisons*** (MoI/HMSO, 1941). This pamphlet covers the period from May 1940 to Spring 1941, and tells of the daily life of the scattered groups of men in Iceland (which Britain had peacefully 'invaded' and part occupied), as well as in the Orkneys, Faeroes and Shetland Islands.

Because much of their work was secret, the book could give little idea why the lonely garrisons were there, which must have puzzled early readers. Some of that story, though, began to emerge in later pamphlets, particularly in *Combined Operations* (1943), *The Royal Marines* (1944) and *Arctic War* (1945). However, travels for the book concealed a secondary purpose, for Linklater was instructed to use it as a cover to visit Greenland, to spy out the purpose of installations that the American military had begun to build there. The pamphlet was the only one of War Office's first four to have been written from personal experience by a man on the spot. It was published in August 1941, which makes it one of the earliest, after *The Battle of Britain* certainly, but before *Bomber Command* and *The Battle of Flanders*.

Completion of the pamphlet (well received by the top brass) coincided with the end of Linklater's work at Scapa Flow and, as already mentioned, he was invited to join the War Office PR team. However, he had not long been in his new post when major changes were introduced at the Army PR Directorate. Beith was transferred to important new duties, ostensibly as a civilian. Well-known in USA (he had earlier collaborated with P G Wodehouse and Guy Bolton in their string of Broadway hit musicals, many of which had later toured the States and come to Britain), he was sent across the Atlantic to spearhead the British Government's discreetly forceful PR campaign directed towards capturing American hearts and minds, and bringing Uncle Sam into the war. He was to spend some years there before returning to contribute at least two more pamphlets to HMSO's series. It is worth noting how Beith's policy when Director of Army PR differed from those of his opposite numbers at the other Service Ministries. The pamphlets which appeared, or were in hand, during his tenure all carried their authors' names. None of those which were commissioned by either the Air Ministry or Admiralty were allowed to do so.

From this time onwards, though, Beith's successor at the War Office – Major General Lawson – adopted new methods. He directed that future pamphlets should be compiled by editorial teams, apparently mainly former journalists now in uniform, and new titles were not again to be openly attributed to any author. Those already in the pipeline were allowed to carry their authors' names, though less prominently than under Beith's jurisdiction. Linklater's experiences under the new regime were frustrating, for his pamphlet project in hand was countermanded before its completion (disinterred later, it eventually appeared in 1945, as *Life Blood*), and his next task was quickly snatched away by the Indian Army, who chose another to write it. It appeared in 1942 as *The Tiger Strikes* but the paperback version appears only to have been published in India. Reading between the lines of a volume of Linklater's autobiography, the impression is received that he was not to produce anything else worth recalling during the rest of his time with Army PR – although he was to provide one further pamphlet for CoI/HMSO after he had left the Army (see chapter 8).

One of those pamphlets already in the pipeline when the regime at War Office changed was ***The Campaign in Greece and Crete*** (MoI/HMSO, 1942). Most of the book was written by novelist David Garnett (strangely enough, an officer in the RAF, at Air Ministry PR), although he was not allowed to put his name on its cover or title page. His work, though, is acknowledged in a note on the verso of the half-title. Garnett had actually learned to fly at his own expense, and obtained a civil pilot's licence in order to make himself more valuable when he volunteered for the RAF – but the Service considered him too old for aircrew and more valuable on terra firma.

The struggle in Greece was a strange episode, its development apparently influenced more by the rules of cricket than by those of war. Even in 1942, Garnett was able to write that the sending of an expeditionary force to Greece had the superficial appearance of a political decision based upon sentimentality. In April 1939, the British Government, in order to discourage further German expansion after their seizure of Czechoslovakia, had guaranteed the independence and integrity of Greece. Italy later (October 1940), in a botched attempt at invading Greece, got itself into desperate trouble, and thus obliged the Germans to bail it out, if only to protect Nazi interests in Romania and Bulgaria. In fact the political situation was much more complex, as Garnett took the trouble to explain, in his pamphlet. It was the old story of 'trouble in the Balkans' yet again.

The Greeks had asked only for help from the RAF, which was given. They had specifically pleaded that British soldiers should not be sent, and that plea had been reinforced by Britain's General Staff, and by General Wavell in Libya, who would have to supply any that were to be sent. The reasons given were, firstly, that sending British troops would precipitate a German invasion of Greece; secondly, that such invasion could not be withstood, so that those sent would inevitably be lost. The Cabinet read the advice – and ordered Wavell to send his best troops!

Within weeks, Wavell's weakened army had been thrown out of Libya, and the Royal Navy had to evacuate the British, first from

Greece, then from Crete, both of which ended up in German hands. There was a further loss of desperately needed battle-hardened men and valuable equipment. It seemed like France all over again.

But nothing is ever as simple as it seems, and the Cabinet had reasons that it could not then reveal. Garnett was able to give some of them, and others emerged later. Thanks to a British and Empire presence aiding a gallant defence by the Greeks, all of whom gave good account of themselves, the Germans also lost great numbers of soldiers, aircrews and their planes. Strategically, the campaign diverted effort from preparing the German invasion of Russia, and that delay led inevitably to far greater German losses. It had all been a chess game on a gigantic board, with the purpose of moves revealed only as the contest unfolded. Tactically, the campaign ended in the expected disappointment and local disaster, but the strategic gains elsewhere were to prove immeasurably vital. How much was political foresight, and how much was luck, of course, we shall never know. But, despite military muddle and some inept leadership, it remains a glorious episode of gallant sacrifice in pursuit of a greater cause.

The Greek adventure was never seen as more than a sideshow to the main event. Churchill had insisted that the Desert Campaigns in North Africa should hold centre-stage, and would be the starting point for the eventual defeat of the Axis (the German, Italian and Japanese alliance). Several times, he was to veto the diversion of British-led effort to other theatres of operations, and even managed to carry President Roosevelt with him, against strongest American advice, to secure the invasion of Tunisia in late 1942. Indeed, Churchill's determination in that regard generated considerable strains upon the American side of the Anglo-American alliance. Not surprisingly, then, the struggle in North (and East) Africa was well covered by HMSO's series of pamphlets. All but one of the resulting books appear to have been team-written, in accord with the new PR policy at War Office.

First in sequence (though not first to appear) was ***The Abyssinian Campaigns*** (MoI/HMSO, 1942), the official story of the conquest of the Italian empire in East Africa, which covers the period from June 1940 to December 1941. There had been great public sympathy for the people of Abyssinia (now Ethiopia), who had suffered much brutality at the hands of their Italian invaders before WW2. The contrasts between invaders and invaded seemed almost those between the new technological age and the Stone Age. Many of the Abyssinian fighters had little more than bows and arrows with which to counter Italian machine guns, bombs and poison gas. When the time shortly arrived for the Italians to be given some of their own medicine, there was much gleeful rejoicing!

Here was military success on a spectacular scale, long overdue after the grim retreats from Norway, France and Greece, and the anxiety of the long-threatened invasion of Britain itself. But the newspaper and newsreel reports, seen from home, made it all seem to have been so easy that it was difficult to see the huge Italian army and air force as a serious enemy, and impossible not to laugh at the buffoon-like posturing of their leader. Our forces in East Africa must surely have felt that they received far less acclaim and honour than had been rightly due to them. Over enormous distances and impossible terrain, and with ludicrously small resources, they had rapidly achieved a triumph of epic proportions. Yet it was quickly forgotten in the pressure of events. And who remembers it, today? This pamphlet, and the next to appear, deserve better from posterity.

Sequentially, the next was ***The Destruction of an Army*** (MoI/HMSO, dated 1941 though possibly not on general sale until 1942). It covers the first campaign in Libya, from September 1940 to February 1941, fought over a desert the size of India. General Wavell's Army of the Nile had been provided and equipped to protect the Suez Canal – but given responsibilities that extended over much of the Middle East. Thanks to Axis control of the Mediterranean, it could only be supplied by the long sea route around Africa, a haul of some 12,000 U-boat infested miles. Its adversary was a huge and expensively equipped Italian army, supported by a large air force and one of the world's most modern navies. It was the battle of David and Goliath fought again – with much the same result.

Wavell's army countered the Italian advance, turned the tide, and swept all before it. As well as those enemy soldiers it killed or seriously wounded, in two months it took over 133,000 prisoners. Vast quantities of equipment were captured, much of it being sent on to the Greek Army, and so turned against its former owners. Reeling from what has been described as 'one of the most remarkable feats of arms in history', Italy then suffered the further humiliation of having General Rommel and his Afrika Korps sent to their rescue. It was at that point that the victorious Wavell was ordered to detach his best units, knowingly sending them to an inevitable fate in Greece, and so leaving all the ground he had just taken inadequately defended. Rommel at once seized the advantage and, within weeks, all Wavell's land gains had been lost and his victorious army had been thrown back, almost to the gates of Cairo. It was a moment of supreme irony. A lesser man would have been broken in heart and spirit – but Wavell was not a lesser man.

The war in North Africa, despite the appearance of the hour, was far from over, and triumphs still to come would feature in further pamphlets. In the meantime, though, a sidelight upon the campaign was to be shown by ***They Sought Out Rommel*** (MoI/HMSO, 1942). Perhaps because the book's story was compiled from a personal diary, contrary to policy its author's name was allowed to appear (though, again, not on its cover or title page). Captain Sean Fielding, fighting with the Green Howards, was given the PR task of conducting a small party of newspaper correspondents into the imminent battle to recover Libya. The War Office had taken care not only to ensure that press men were at the ringside in time for round one, but that they should have the best seats throughout the fight.

Fielding kept his party so much in the thick of battle that, to change the metaphor, sometimes they ran so far with the leading hounds that they had to dodge the Desert Fox, Rommel. In a terrain so featureless that maps were meaningless, they navigated by the sound of gunfire, often unsure whether the cloud of dust they chased would turn out to be that of friend or foe. The book covers a mere forty-six days, during which the correspondents were kept at the heart of events thanks, they acknowledged, to the zeal, foresight, courage and energy of their conducting officer. As well as providing an insight into a major battle, the book reveals the methods and risks of collecting the news for a hungrily-waiting world outside.

The record of the overall campaign continued with ***The Battle of Egypt*** (MoI/HMSO, 1943), covering the period from June to November 1942, taking the record up to the point where the enemy had again been cleared out of Egypt – in other words, a return pretty much to the status quo of early 1940, before Wavell's Libyan campaign. That great work still had to be repeated. The publication itself consciously broke new ground, for it was not so much a 'pamphlet' but more a magazine. In appearance it was very much like one of those wartime mass circulation weeklies – *Illustrated* for example. Similar editorial techniques had been used for its preparation and design, and it had even been printed on Odhams' magazine presses at Watford. The impression is clearly given that it

'The breaking of the Afrika Korps.' Reprinted from* The Eighth Army *(MoI/HMSO, 1944)

had been decided to target a new, wider market, and that the job had been handed to already proven experts in that field.

That story was to be both expanded in detail and extended in reach by the next in sequence, ***The Eighth Army*** (MoI/HMSO, 1944), a substantial paperback of 104 large pages which must have sold in positively enormous numbers, for it is still one of the two titles most often seen, fifty years later (the other is *Front Line,* MoI/HMSO, 1942). The book covers the period from September 1941 to January 1943 and by the time it appeared on the bookstalls the following year, readers were beginning to feel confident that the war's tide was flowing strongly in favour of the Allies. For, by then, the events covered by its sequel, ***Tunisia*** (MoI/HMSO, 1944) were already known. The Axis powers had been finally and decisively ejected from North Africa, and Italy itself had been successfully invaded.

Tunisia repeated the apparently successful format first adopted by *The Eighth Army*, and is magazine-style, with much of its space taken up by news photographs with captions, its explanatory texts remaining comparatively short. Thus its main strength is its graphic illustrations, gripping and evocative. As the story it tells begins with the joint American and British landings (largely unopposed) in North-West Africa in late 1942, perforce it tells nothing of the dramatic story of the assembling of the vast force needed – that was still secret at the time of its publication. Happily, part of that complicated and immense effort of transportation of men and equipment was later to be revealed in a pamphlet that will figure in chapter 7. Hundreds of ships took part, mustered, loaded and despatched from dozens of ports, all in complete secrecy. In Britain, the railways coordinated the delivery, loading and routeing of 1,600 trains filled with men and equipment, for carefully scheduled arrival at docks around the country, and rapid embarkation. Any delay in arrival or dispersal threatened secrecy and invited attack, yet the whole, vast operation was carried out without any apparent hitch. The preparations for the invasion of Tunisia thus provided a dramatic dress rehearsal for the Normandy landings as well as representing the opening of the final act of the long North African struggle.

The Home Front's long-sustained campaign against the Luftwaffe was recorded, in part, in the jointly-sponsored ***Roof Over Britain*** (MoI/HMSO, 1943). The War Office and Air Ministry combined resources to compile this record of the anti-aircraft defence of Great Britain, from 1939 to 1942. The C-in-C of Anti-Aircraft Command, General Sir Frederick Pile, stated in his book *'Ack-Ack* (Harrap, 1949), that HMSO's pamphlet had been prepared by the Public Relations department of his Command, but the British Library Catalogue attributes authorship to Anthony Cotterell, a serving officer who wrote several wartime books. Perhaps Cotterell was a member of General Pile's PR team, and led this project. The pamphlet's striking cover, with its bold artwork, was by the Army's poster artist, Abram Games, famous during the war for the vigorous imagery of his official work.

The period covered by the pamphlet was, as General Pile was later to confess, a time when his gunners were poorly equipped, and the best-trained of their colleagues had been detached to fight elsewhere. AA gunnery was a new science that had to be learned by doing, and its best successes were still in an unknown future. The book explains the complexities of identifying distant planes;

predicting their likely courses, speeds and heights; and relaying estimated data to the right gunsites, who then had to lay their guns accurately and fire them at the precise second that would deliver the shells over several miles to explode in proximity to their targets. No easy task in daylight and with ample time, it had instead to be accomplished in the dark and under pressure, in all weathers. Gunsites were often manned by a mixture of men who were neither young nor fit enough for the infantry; by women; and later by the Home Guard.

In view of the difficulties and inadequacies it was, perhaps, a wonder that they achieved so much – three times they shot down over fifty planes in a single week, once over seventy; on one occasion, the number of guns defending London was doubled in twenty-four hours. In fact, when enemy records came to be examined after the war, AA Command's score was revised sharply upwards to include many kills at first attributed to the RAF. In his text, Cotterell included the work of the searchlight and balloon units, and of the Royal Observer Corps, but was unable to refer at all to the aid given by radar. When reading the pamphlet, it is as well to remember that only the first half of a longer story was recounted here. Cotterell also wrote another pamphlet-length text which ought to have been in HMSO's series, but somehow it escaped to be published commercially as a slim hardback (see chapter 7).

Two unit histories fall within this chapter, though the first, ***By Air to Battle*** (MoI/HMSO, 1945), was actually sponsored not by the War Office but by the Air Ministry. Possibly that may have been because it had been written by our old friend, Hilary Saunders, whom we last met at the time of his transfer to Combined Operations HQ. This was the story of the British First and Sixth Airborne Divisions, 1940–1945 (and Saunders went on to write full-length histories both of the Commandos and of the Parachute Regiment, published by Michael Joseph in 1949 and 1950, respectively).

The success of the Airborne Divisions is a refutation of the allegation that the British may often be late-starters but are sometimes quick learners! A mistaken impression is that, after being taken somewhat at a disadvantage by the Germans' use of parachute troops in their invasion of Crete in 1941, the British thought that they had better look into the matter, in case there might be something in it. In fact, first to use parachute troops had been the Russians, during manoeuvres in 1936, when one of the foreign observers there had been General Wavell. The same year, Goering began the organisation of German airborne forces, though a similar start in Britain was not made until late June 1940. Only some seven months later, on 10 February 1941, British airborne troops went into battle in Southern Italy – and that was a couple of months before the Germans attacked Greece!

The other unit history is ***The Royal Armoured Corps*** (HMSO, 1945 – MoI made no claim to involvement), jointly written by Frank Owen and H W Atkins. Frank Owen's is a famous name in Army PR. A former senior journalist, he had been prominent in SE Asia Command's PR effort, and had produced newspapers for the troops that had been dropped, daily, to units scattered widely around the Far East. The pamphlet's striking cover artwork by Eric Kennington (T E Lawrence's illustrator) is, strangely, dated 1943, so its appearance on this pamphlet was perhaps a second use. Armoured fighting vehicles had been visualised long before they loomed, via tractor-technology, out of the dawn mist at the Battle of the Somme on 15 September 1916 – indeed, the idea of the tank is almost as old as warfare itself. However, it was not until WW2 that they finally shook off myth and emerged as a fearsome force in their own right. Owen and Atkins' pamphlet first provides an overview of the development and early use of tanks before detailing the conversion of a civilian (or a cavalry-man) into a Royal Armoured Corps warrior. The second half explains the current use of tanks in modern warfare. Though the book was produced for general sale, it would also have been a most useful basic training aid for newly recruited RAC troops.

The War Office's contribution to the HMSO series may seem rather short and patchy, particularly as it contains little that deals with the later stages of the war, when the Army had stopped suffering defeats and enduring evacuations, and had scored a succession of impressive victories that had taken the battles right across enemy-held Europe into Germany itself. That patchiness is a great pity, but the Allied Armies will figure substantially in later chapters, in records sponsored by authorities other than the War Office.

'Replacing the tank track. The driver needs the whole crew for this job.'
Reprinted from* The Royal Armoured Corps *(HMSO, 1945)

Chapter 4

Admiralty

The Silent Service Speaks

Traditionally 'the silent service' from the outset the Royal Navy had held firmly to the view that news of Services' activities should not be officially released, and that the inconvenient initiatives of journalists who nonetheless sought it out should be subject to the strictest censorship. The censorship division of MoI contained a strong contingent of naval staff, who were left in no doubt of the views of their superiors at the Admiralty, and who were thus at first ruthlessly dedicated to preventing the escape of war news.

The PR successes of the early pamphlets from the War Office and the Air Ministry were looked upon disdainfully by the Admiralty, who saw them as naught but an unseemly scramble to curry favour amongst the uninformed, and beneath the dignity of a Service with a proper amount of tradition and self-confidence. No doubt the admirals were still grinding their teeth about the escape into print in 1940 of ***The Battle of the River Plate*** (see chapter 1). At least that had not been a specially written pamphlet like those embarrassing puffs issued on behalf of the Army and Royal Air Force; that had been a mere compilation of extracts from official reports, which could be explained away as tempering the line-shooting excesses of the newspaper hacks. Navy silence might well have continued for much longer had it not been for a strange incident.

Those were still the early days of aircraft carriers, the first examples of which had been but conversions of more traditional vessels. However, in 1935, the Navy had ordered a purpose-built aircraft carrier, HMS *Ark Royal*, which had entered service in November 1938. Building the *Ark Royal* had been the most valuable contract the Admiralty had issued in twenty years, and it was to be the longest ship ever built on Merseyside. Her flight deck was 800 ft long. The ship rose through nine decks; could sail at over 30 knots; had a crew of 1,575; and could stay at sea for six months, if needed. This was a modern ship with a very high profile indeed in a navy which – though large by comparison with the navies of other nations – included more than a fair share of ships which were old or obsolescent.

Within a few weeks of the outbreak of war, the *Ark Royal*, in company with other ships, came under air attack. The raiders were beaten off, but one of the Luftwaffe pilots reported on landing that he had dive-bombed the *Ark Royal*, and thought he might have hit it. (In fact, the *Ark* had changed course in time, and his single bomb had missed, the only damage sustained being some broken crockery.) He made no claim to have sunk the ship, but the Nazi Propaganda Ministry, without referring the matter to Goebbels, promptly made that claim for him. Suddenly, the pilot was manipulated by the state-controlled media into the status of national hero.

Such was the resulting media lionisation of the embarrassed pilot that it soon became politically necessary for him to be decorated and promoted, though both the High Command and he well knew that the claims made on his behalf by the propagandists were false – as did his fellow pilots, who made him a laughing stock. Goebbels, too, soon learned that his Ministry's early claim had been not just false (he could live with that) but unsustainable to boot. But by then, so intense had been the propaganda effort that he dared not retract, and German radio stations continued to plug the false victory. At home, it led to an ironic catch phrase, 'where is the *Ark Royal*?', which rivalled for popularity those of radio comedians. The *Ark* continued to fight on, very publicly, off Norway, in the Atlantic and the Mediterranean until in November 1941 she was torpedoed while in sight of Gibraltar, and began to sink. Apart from one man killed in the first explosion, all the crew were rescued, but the ship was lost – a fact which was promptly announced from London, and used greatly to the further embarrassment of Dr Goebbels.

It is to the credit of MoI that they were able to use this incident at

The Merseyside launching of HMS* Ark Royal. *Throughout its three years of service with the Royal Navy, the ship was seldom out of the headlines, a focus of propaganda and controversy.
Photograph reprinted from* Ark Royal *(MoI/HMSO, 1942)

last to lure the Admiralty out of their stubborn silence, thanks in no small part to the presence of Captain Henry Taprell Dorling, RN (the well-known writer on naval affairs, 'Taffrail') who had earlier been brought from retirement to stiffen Navy representation at MoI. Although the resulting pamphlet, ***Ark Royal*** (MoI/HMSO, 1942), was to be anonymous, the Admiralty would have been hard put to muster any sustainable objection to it being written by such a respected and qualified author, and one of their own. So, the Admiralty's first offering eventually appeared in October 1942, in company with the War Office's sixth, *The Highland Division*, and the Air Ministry's fourth, *Bomber Command Continues.*

The opportunity was not missed to rub Dr Goebbels' nose further into the mess his Ministry had made in 1939 so that the loss of a capital ship had been turned into not one, but a series of three propaganda triumphs. Although Taffrail never acknowledged authorship of this pamphlet by name, he did later reveal that he had written 'several' (i.e. certainly more than two) for HMSO's series, one of which we know without doubt was *The Battle of the Atlantic*, and his authorship of *Ark Royal* was considered amongst reviewers at the time to be an open secret.

During his thirty years active service with the fleet, Taffrail had served around the world, and had spent WW1 mainly in destroyers serving in the North Sea. Afterwards, he had spent a while on the Admiralty staff and, after his release from MoI, was to return to sea and be involved with the landings in North Africa in 1942. Between these two spells, he had established himself as a successful author and journalist. Having such impeccable credentials must have helped considerably to persuade the Admiralty to allow him to be their mouthpiece on this occasion.

It may well have been Nazi propaganda that convinced the Admiralty of a need for their next pamphlet though, if so, it appeared somewhat belatedly. The Italians had called the Mediterranean 'our sea', and had claimed to have bottled-up the Royal Navy in the Eastern Mediterranean, where it was alleged to have been grievously constricted and short of supplies, at the mercy of the home-based and numerically strong Italian air force and its theoretically powerful modern fleet. Such claims were contemptuously dismissed in ***East of Malta, West of Suez*** (MoI/HMSO, 1943), which gave an account of the naval war in that theatre from September 1939 to March 1941. It was written by another popular author on naval affairs, Paymaster Captain Lewis Ritchie, RN (better recognised as 'Bartimeus', the blind beggar, whom he chose to provide his pseudonym as whimsical commentary upon the poor eyesight that had condemned him to the administrative branch of the Navy). Ritchie had been a staff officer in WW1, and in WW2 had served briefly in naval intelligence and been present at Dunkirk before being lent to MoI.

The pamphlet's record includes the story of the decisive night-time Battle of Matapan, off Greece, when three Italian cruisers and two destroyers were seen to have been sunk, and other important Italian ships, after sustaining damage, limped off into the darkness, never again to be seen afloat. One Italian ship surrendered without firing a shot, while another shelled its own consorts. The battle also had the later effect of discouraging Italy from intervening in the desperate operations surrounding the evacuations from Greece and Crete. This allegedly bottled-up Royal Navy made possible the successful campaigns in Abyssinia and Syria, which in turn denied the Germans any hopes of reaching India from the West and so linking with the Japanese. This is the only one of the pamphlets dealing with the work of the Royal Navy that had the distinction of achieving a US edition, being published in hardback in New York, in 1944.

'Bartimeus' continued the story in ***The Mediterranean Fleet*** (MoI/HMSO, 1944), which covered the period from April 1941 to January 1943, up to the capture of Tripoli, and the Royal Navy's resumption of command of the great sea route through the Mediterranean. What a pity that this part of the series' record of events was not extended just a little further, which would have enabled it to include the surrender, at Malta, of the remaining units of the Italian Navy. The Royal Navy never did develop much of a

The return from Greece – of the lucky ones. The unlucky were to spend four years in captivity. Photograph reprinted from **The Mediterranean Fleet** *(MoI/HMSO, 1944)*

taste for blowing its own bugle in concerts organised by MoI, generally preferring to limit itself to telling of aspects of its responsibilities rather than painting broad canvases of whole campaigns.

Of course, it is only too easy to take too simplistic a view of the versions of events set out in official publications. These MoI/HMSO pamphlets were designed for a purpose, which they filled superbly at the time, and they have a more lasting value both as reminder of what had been the contemporary view and as a 'first draft of history'. Interesting and useful though they are, it remains important not to invest them with merits to which they could never aspire – and never claimed. None of the pamphlets told the whole story. They were too short to do so; their writers did not know the whole story; and some of the aspects their writers did know could not be told at the time for security reasons.

When they were written, no one knew the full story behind events, for it was not until after the war, when enemy records could be compared with those of the Allies, that a whole picture could begin to emerge. Even at the time they were written, not even the War Cabinet and the Chiefs of Staff were as well-informed as can be the humblest reader today, thanks to post-war research. The achievements of commanders and their forces can now, sometimes, be seen to have been first set down in a way that history was later to contradict. It had all happened before, in WW1, and that it would again prove to be the case was fully realised by those at the Admiralty at the start of WW2, so it would be surprising if that knowledge was not at least a factor in their reluctance to enter the PR war. For our part, we should not, from the disdainful heights of hindsight, sneer at such early records. Rather, we should continue to marvel that the men on the spot achieved so much with so little, misdirected from above and misinformed from below as, unavoidably, they so often were.

The next five titles are all examples of the Navy's preference to record for MoI use aspects of their responsibilities rather than to detail campaigns. First of them was ***Fleet Air Arm*** (MoI/HMSO, 1943), the Admiralty's account of naval air organisation and operations, from its resumption of control from the RAF in 1938 to the landings in North Africa in November 1942. The book is

particularly interesting for its accounts of the development of aircraft carriers, the training of fleet pilots, and the difficulties of flying on operations from a moving base which must conceal its constantly changing position from the enemy. Not only does a naval pilot have to find and attack a heavily defended target, but he has to save enough fuel and time, and have the wit to navigate, in order to return, perhaps injured and in a damaged aircraft, to his carrier which will have several times changed course and speed, and perhaps be a hundred miles away from where he left it.

For some years, this pamphlet was thought to have been written by John Cecil Moore, the well-known broadcaster and writer on rural life and fishing, who was a serving Fleet Air Arm pilot when it was published. Moore did indeed write a book of just that title, but that was a hardback, commercially published the same year. However, the John Moore Society, with benefit of full access to Moore's wartime letters home, and diaries, has been unable to find any confirming evidence that he wrote *Fleet Air Arm*. They have been able to establish, though, that Moore did write the next title: ***The Navy and the Y Scheme*** (HMSO, 1944). MoI seems not to have been involved, perhaps because of the pamphlet's special purpose. The 'Y Scheme' was designed to provide pre-entry training for those who would want to join the Navy and, for those who did well, it provided a guarantee of acceptance into the aspirant's preferred branch as a sailor, airman or marine, but with a fast track to a commission for those with aptitude. The pamphlet was written for the particular purpose of providing useful information for such potential recruits, with much detailed advice and information, but was – and is – nonetheless of lasting general interest as a unique snapshot of life in the Royal Navy in 1944.

Appearing around the same time was ***The Royal Marines***

(MoI/HMSO, 1944). Although sub-titled 'the Admiralty's account of their achievement 1939–1943', it also provided a potted history of the Corps and its naval role since its inception in 1664, as well as a record of their specialist services in WW2. In all, a more rounded and detailed account than was usual in the series. The Marines' story is not confined to this title alone, but is also covered in part elsewhere in the series, particularly though not exclusively in *The Northern Garrisons* and *Combined Operations*. The pamphlet also provides some information upon actions that do not, themselves, figure separately in the series – Norway and Singapore for example.

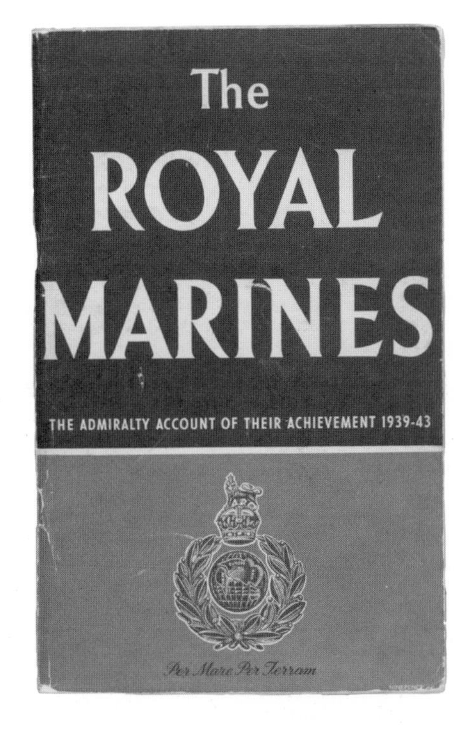

A second contribution almost certainly from 'Taffrail', although similarly unacknowledged by name by him, was ***His Majesty's Minesweepers*** (MoI/HMSO, 1943). Taffrail had been a specialist in mine warfare, and had previously written a history of the subject, published shortly before the war began. Thus, well grounded, he was able to make a fascinating story for HMSO's series about what might seem a somewhat unlikely area for a popular pamphlet. His text opened with a history of the use of sea mines, and of minelaying (rather surprisingly beginning in 1585), before detailing the organisation of modern counter-measures and operations from August 1939.

Minesweeping was one area of defence where Britain really was prepared from the outset. Until new and purpose-built vessels could come into use, its large fishing fleet could immediately provide for requisition an abundance of suitable vessels complete with crews experienced in their handling (which, incidentally, goes a long way to explain the wartime's chronic shortage of unrationed fresh fish). There already existed an invaluable nucleus of reserve officers and ratings with practical knowledge of the techniques required. Thus, an augmented fleet was on its war stations before the end of August, 1939. Even so, new challenges were shortly to be presented, with the deployments of Hitler's threatened 'secret weapons'. The causes of unexplained sinkings had to be analysed and tracked down, and samples of the new magnetic and acoustic mines recovered to be taken apart at great peril, so that their mechanisms could be understood and new methods of defence devised. Theirs was to prove a world-wide, years-long, cat-and-mouse game, that stretched courage to the limit, taking and saving many lives. The story of minesweeping proved to be far more complex, dramatic and exciting than it might at first have appeared to the uninformed.

More obviously dramatic would have been ***His Majesty's Submarines*** (MoI/HMSO, 1945). Everyone thought they knew the tensions, dangers and excitements of a submariner's life, shown many times in cinema films, and reported upon in the wartime press. The reality, however, was somewhat less cinematic, and the Admiralty would only rarely allow correspondents to go to sea in submarines to find out, for the excellent reasons that their needs for air and support would imperil crew-members in an emergency. Also, much of submarine operations had previously to be kept secret until this book could take advantage of the approaching end of the war to provide a wide-ranging account of the work of the submarine service up to late 1944. The book's illustrations give a graphic impression of the narrow, cramped circumstances of life in a slender, enclosed hull. The tensions and the dangers have to be imagined.

The final pamphlet to carry Admiralty endorsement was not to appear until a year after the war was over. That was the official account of the fight against the U-boats, ***The Battle of the Atlantic***

(CoI/HMSO, 1946), and was jointly sponsored with the Air Ministry. This is the one pamphlet that Taffrail openly acknowledged having written, and we must be grateful that preparation and publication were delayed until a fuller story could be revealed. Taffrail was an ideal choice for its author, and this long pamphlet (104 pages, all dedicated to text and essential maps) shows all the signs of his renowned accuracy, close attention to detail and clarity of exposition.

'A midget submarine, on the surface.' Reprinted from* His Majesty's Submarines *(MoI/HMSO, 1945)

He had an amazing story to tell, and he told it well. The Battle of the Atlantic raged, uninterrupted, for sixty-eight months, beginning less than twelve hours after the declaration of war and not ending until Grand Admiral Doenitz's signal to his U-boats to cease hostilities and return to base, sent on 4 May 1945. Even then, a handful of German submarines escaped to Japan, with the intention of fighting on. Until the very end, the German U-boat arm fought with determination, discipline and efficiency, without relaxation or hesitancy to incur risks. Indeed, on the night before Germany's surrender, two merchant ships were sunk near the Firth of Forth and a minesweeper was sunk in Lyme Bay. The U-boats came close to winning their battle and, though its continuance became increasingly difficult for them, they were never defeated at sea. It was the Allies' capture of the bases to which U-boats needed to return to refuel and rearm that forced an end to their campaign.

It has been argued that the rest of the war had been carried on the back of the Battle of the Atlantic for, had the Allies lost that, the Germans might well not have lost to the Russians and might have been victorious elsewhere. Churchill had made an early forecast, that only the RAF could win the war for Britain, but only the Royal Navy could lose it, in the Atlantic. Both parts of that forecast were to be fully tested by events.

Compared to the chapters dealing with those pamphlets sponsored by the Air Ministry and War Office, the taciturn Admiralty's crop may seem sparse. The naval story, though, is extended in further pamphlets to be dealt with in later chapters. The Royal Navy had a large and important part to play in the story of *Combined Operations* (1943), and they were joined in the war at sea by (among many others) the Dutch, whose story is told in *Queen Wilhelmina's Navy* (1944), both of which are dealt with in chapter six. Three pamphlets that deal mainly with the Merchant Navy, but in which the Royal Navy had a part, are covered in chapter five. The Royal Navy figures in *Build the Ships* (1946), also in chapter five, and very substantially so in *Science at War* (1947), in chapter eight. These last two pamphlets, in particular, provide fascinating insights into how the Navy came to carry out several of its most difficult tasks so successfully.

Even so, the Navy never quite made up for its late entry into HMSO's series, and the nature of its contributions were mainly rather different from those of its companion Services. Strangely, though, there is a marked uniformity in design, page size and appearance that is generally absent from those pamphlets sponsored by the Air Ministry and the War Office. It is tempting to imagine that, unlike those Ministries, the Admiralty might actually have seen its pamphlets as a succession of titles that would build into a series. However, it is unlikely that Admiralty staff would have concerned themselves much with design or been provided with any opportunity to do so. That would clearly have been the province of HMSO who, unfortunately, have no archives that might throw some light upon how Admiralty-sponsored pamphlets achieved the pleasing and sensible uniformity that mostly eluded those from all the other sources.

Chapter 5

Home Front

Civilians at War

In Summer 1939, the political situation in Britain was, in some respects, the opposite of that within Germany. There, a well-prepared Nazi Party, Government and armed forces had long been itching for a war that its citizens did not want. In Britain, on the other hand, the people had become disillusioned with a genuine, but apparently doomed, political effort to avoid war. The weight of public opinion was pushing a reluctant and still under-prepared Government into a war that it was desperate to avoid – or at least to postpone for a year or two.

Those who should have been the nation's leaders during the 1930s had largely been wiped out in the carnage of WW1, which had left Britain with a Government made up of tired and elderly men, cautious survivors, and artful failures, who had neglected to rebuild or revitalise the country. However, despite timid politicians, the home economy was at last beginning to emerge from years of depression. This slow climb out of financial stringency towards solvency left the Government nervous about raising taxes to fund preparations for war, but many outside Government, convinced that war was unavoidable, made personal efforts to prepare, and persuaded others to do the same. Much of what they were doing, though, had to be kept out of sight at such a vulnerable stage for fear that, if recognised for what it was, it might be stopped by anxious authorities.

In fact, preparations both official and unofficial had been in hand, in some instances since 1934, only months after Hitler's coming to power; before the Nazi take-over of Austria; and well before Germany's march into Czechoslovakia in Spring 1939. Although Parliament had been reluctant to provide cash for weapons development and for rearming, much that could be done by personal initiative, by massaging budgets and by cash-free goodwill, had been done – often in spite of officially-imposed obstruction. The civil development programmes of both the Spitfire and especially the Hurricane are cases in point.

Government signally failed to recognise the mood of the people, both before war began and throughout its early months, doubting their will both to endure the return to hardship that would result from a new fight against aggression, and to make the essential sacrifices for a cause that could be believed in. When the war did at last begin, in Britain at least it took an entirely unexpected form – almost nothing at all appeared to happen!

On Sunday, 3 September 1939, the Prime Minister informed the nation by radio broadcast that a state of war existed between Britain and Germany. People had been expecting that war would begin with massive air raids on the undefended cities, and so were not surprised that, shortly after the Prime Minister's broadcast, the air raid sirens sounded. This was going to be it! But, instead of the skies darkening with a vast air armada that rained bombs indiscriminately, nothing happened. Well, not much.

What had happened was that a single plane had been detected, approaching the South Coast. Although first plotted and tracked by a hundred technicians, and then observed by a thousand pairs of eyes, it remained unidentified. The Army, the RAF, Civil Defence, Police, Fire and Ambulance services were called to the alert. When it became clear that the plane was on a course for London, the air raid sirens were sounded across the South East, and a flight of Spitfires was scrambled to intercept it. Before they could do so, the solitary plane circled, south of London, and made a leisurely landing at Croydon. It contained two French officers, delegated to attend the Allied air mission in London.

Already, the first contingents of the British Expeditionary Force to France were on the move through South East England to embarkation ports. Their transit, well planned in advance, was conducted so circumspectly that hardly anyone was aware that a small army had passed like a shadow through the mist. Throughout the country, regular and reserve servicemen, mostly in civilian

clothes, were travelling, called or recalled to their units. Out of sight, the anthill was seething but, on the surface, all seemed calm. Life was to go on like that, with little to see and little reported, for several months. It was not until the few, frantic weeks before the fall of France in Spring 1940, that war seemed to acquire much reality for Britons still going about their normal lives. The threat of invasion from the recently captured French ports changed everything. Now, every Briton was close to the Front and, indeed, many were in the frontline itself.

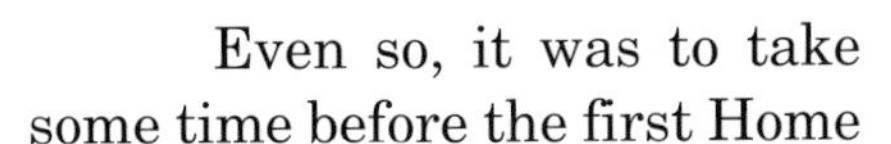

Even so, it was to take some time before the first Home Front paperback appeared in HMSO's series. That was ***Front Line*** (MoI/HMSO, 1942), sponsored by the Ministry of Home Security. A substantial paperback – 160 large pages – it told of Civil Defence in Britain up to December 1941. Its comprehensiveness was reflected in its price, a substantial 2s, the most expensive yet.

Written by journalist S C Leslie, *Front Line* clearly sold in vast numbers despite its price, for it is amongst the most commonly found titles today. Unfortunately, it is seldom found in good condition, because of its flimsy paper cover, which does little to protect its contents. It is also prone to shedding leaves from the inside. It is not a narrative of organisation, but of action, though depersonalised by the understandable decision to omit names from the stories told.

The book reminds us that the first bomb did not fall until 17 October 1939, on Hoy in the Orkneys, that it took until 16 March 1940 before the first civilian was killed – coincidentally, also in the Orkneys. The first bombs on the mainland fell near Canterbury, on 9 May, with the first attack on an industrial area not until 24 May, at Middlesborough. No bombs at all fell in or around

Reprinted from **Front Line** ***(MoI/HMSO, 1942)***

London until 18 June, when the war had been under way for over nine months. However, the Luftwaffe soon made up for its slow start to the long-expected attacks upon civilians and their homes. What the book could not record (it was not known until later) was that, despite such a slow start, up to the end of 1942, more civilians had been killed by the enemy than had servicemen and women. Clearly, once the German attacks on Britain did get under way from their new bases in occupied France, it quickly became an intensive and remorseless campaign, with wide effects.

Among the workaday civilian activities most grievously affected by the bombing was the transport industry, whose story up to early 1942 is told in ***Transport Goes to War*** (MoI/HMSO, 1942) sponsored by the Ministry of War Transport. Even without air attack, their work would have been much harder, due to all the military movements, greatly increased industrial output and more people needing transport to and from work, at all hours. For best protection, a greater proportion of seaborne traffic was arriving and leaving via west coast ports, which meant that road and rail routes had to be reorganised, facilities expanded and staff relocated. (For an idea of the extent of that work and its effect upon the oil industry, see chapter 7.) All that work had to be done subject to security, in the blackout, and under bombing. Lorries, locomotives and rolling stock were liable to be destroyed, while roads, tracks and signalling systems had to be repaired under greatly-increased pressure, using resources that were getting ever scarcer; many new lines and sidings, tunnels and embankments had to be constructed, operated and maintained for new military bases and war factories.

As well as carrying out their normal – though greatly increased – duties, transport workers also had to act as fire-fighters, rescue and first aid personnel, and do their share of fire watching. Amazingly, they were also among the most enthusiastic and active Home Guards. Many hundreds of them were killed and thousands injured, carrying out their civilian duties. Pre-war, throughout the transport industry, there had been a culture of competition between thousands of rival bus and lorry companies and between the four main railway networks, and their schedules and routes had been organised to individual advantage. Almost overnight, all of that had to be changed, with cooperation and coordination becoming the new

watch-words. Thus, the organisational and operational changes throughout this complex industry were vast, reaching into literally every corner of every yard, station, dock, canal, garage and bus depot. It was accomplished quickly and well through a determination never to let down the fighting men.

A part of the story that could not be told at that stage because it was secret, was that the railways and London Transport were also using their engineering facilities to boost war production: the railways were actually building tanks, planes and boats for the Services (see chapter 7).

None of this effort, and comparable efforts in other industries, could have been carried through without complete mobilisation of civilians, including bringing into work those who would otherwise have stayed at home. The Ministry of Labour and National Service sponsored ***Manpower*** (MoI/HMSO, 1944), the story of Britain's mobilisation for war. Literally the whole nation, excepting only the very young and very old, was put onto a war footing in the shortest possible time. In an instance of the apocryphal 'chicken or egg' conundrum, J B Priestley, who the same year wrote a novel about an aircraft factory (*Daylight on Saturday*), was chosen to write this detailed account of a difficult subject.

Government and workers were fortunate to have as long-term Minister of Labour the highly-respected, capable and tough trade union leader, Ernest Bevin. In the need to persuade free citizens to surrender for the duration their hard-fought-for rights, Bevin was able to carry workers and their leaders along with his thinking, and to show by the consistency of his personal efforts that he was worthy of their trust. It helped also that he could be seen to have the vision to know what was needed and strength of character to get it.

What Bevin accomplished was to establish and operate a system for the recruiting and control of labour far more intensive and comprehensive than Germany's, yet which never wandered towards the slave labour methods shamelessly adopted by the enemy. It was thus accepted as fair, and broadly supported by unions and workers alike. Although labour disputes were by no means unknown, the system was a tremendous achievement, kept effective by a system of compulsion and controls, checks and balances, that reached down into every corner of civil life.

The quiet heroism of the merchant seamen was recorded and honoured both by the series and in the cinema, by ***The Saga of San Demetrio*** (HMSO, 1942), the story of one ship and its crew. It is not entirely clear what might have been the involvement of MoI and the Ministry of War Transport with this publication, but the pamphlet was written by Miss F Tennyson Jesse, who also wrote the screenplay for the film, released in 1943 under the slightly different title of *San Demetrio London*. Unlike the pamphlet, the film was not in documentary form, but was an exciting action film with a cast of well-known actors, but both pamphlet and film at least made it clear that their accounts were compiled from official records and eye-witness accounts by the ship's own officers. Incidentally, this seems to have been the only pamphlet in the series written by a woman.

In October 1940, MV *San Demetrio* sailed from Canada, bound for Britain with a cargo of petrol, in a convoy escorted by HMS *Jervis Bay*, a requisitioned merchant ship that had been fitted with guns and crewed by the Royal Navy. The convoy met up with a German pocket-battleship, and the *Jervis Bay* gallantly sacrificed herself to give the ships in her care a chance to scatter and run. *San Demetrio* was set ablaze by shell-fire, and her crew, unable to control the fires, took to the lifeboats, leaving her to explode and sink in due course.

Strangely, she did not do so, and part of her crew found and reboarded her the next day. To say that they put out the fires, repaired the engines, and got her safely to port in Britain, would be an understatement worthy of the best of the Merchant Service. The few who reboarded her were suffering from exposure and wounds, the damage was difficult to repair, and the ship almost impossible to steer and to keep under way. They were too few, and there was little food fit to eat. That the ship and her cargo were saved was a triumph of leadership, skill and determination. It is a pity that the pamphlet should be so scarce today, and that only a mutilated copy of the film is so seldom shown on TV. Theirs is a story that deserves to be a constant reminder of the bravery and dedication of the merchant crews that kept Britain fed and supplied throughout.

Their story was also a story of neglect and abuse by their employers. John Dancy's biography, *Walter Oakeshott, A Diversity of Gifts* (Michael Russell, 1995), reveals how Oakeshott, at the time High Master of St Paul's School, and occasional member of Admiralty Interview Boards, wangled his way on to a merchant convoy to Nova Scotia in Spring 1943, in return for a promise to provide for the Ministry of War Transport a pamphlet upon the convoy system. That gave an opportunity to compare the seamen's conditions of service on British, American and Norwegian ships sailing in the same convoy, and Oakeshott's manuscript included stinging criticisms of pay and accommodation provided for British crews. His manuscript was deemed unacceptable, and was never published. The Ministry of War Transport had to set about finding another author for the story it wished to lay before the world.

The story of the Merchant Service as a whole appeared in two pamphlets, both in preparation at the same time (1944), yet widely separated by publication dates. First was ***Merchantmen at War*** (MoI/HMSO, 1944), sponsored by the Ministry of War Transport, a 144 large-page pamphlet that gives a detailed account of the deep-water ships, worldwide, and takes their story up to the time of the D-Day landings in France. The book has two poems specially written for it by Poet Laureate, John Masefield, and was written by the novelist, playwright and wartime diarist, J L Hodson. Although published anonymously in Britain, the US edition (with the slightly changed title of *British Merchant Men at War*) carries his name.

Merchant seamen were in the war from the very beginning. The liner *Athenia* was torpedoed only nine hours after hostilities began, and HMSO's pamphlet, *Battle of the Atlantic* (see chapter 4) details the appalling rate of attrition wreaked by the enemy right up to the eve of Germany's surrender. Of all the Services face-to-face with the enemy, the Merchant Service suffered the highest proportion of casualties – nearly a quarter of those engaged – and yet the pamphlet records the amazing statistic that 'for each convoy that has suffered loss since the war started, two or three have reached harbour intact, having overcome ... natural hazards, and ... the perils of mine, submarine torpedo, aerial bomb and shells from the surface raider'.

It is hard to comprehend the extraordinary nature of the Merchant Service. Unlike each of the armed services, it was not a single embodied entity at all. Its ships were almost all privately owned, and a third of them sailed under foreign flags. Their crews were of all nationalities; they included many owners, captains, officers and men who owed no allegiance to Britain and were not legally bound either to serve her interests or accept her directions. Thus, such men were not obligated to hazard their lives, and accept the risks of shipwreck, drowning or mutilation in Britain's service. And yet they did – day in, day out, every voyage, for years on end, seeing the dangers around them and seeing their shipmates die.

The ships they served in were often old, slow and unsafe, their conditions of work harsh and dangerous, and there were few comforts at sea. They worked around the clock, without days off, separated from homes and families. Even for officers, work had been intermittent and insecure for years before the war, and the pay was bad. Once in port, ships were unloaded, turned around, and sent back to sea as quickly as possible, so there was little rest, little relief from the tension of the dangers of their work. Ashore in Britain, they lived in hostels or digs close to the docks, and were thus subjected to the most severe air raids, by day and night. Many survived the perils of the voyage only to be killed ashore. Oswald Preston, the Canadian hero of the *San Demetrio* was never found, believed killed in the bombed wreckage of a dockside seamen's club.

The greatest early augmentation to the size of the merchant fleet had been a direct result of German treachery – a glorious 'own goal'. Germany's underhand invasion of Norway in 1940 resulted in Norway's vast merchant marine – one of the world's largest fleets – deciding not to return home from sea but immediately to join the Allied cause. The Danish and Dutch merchant fleets followed their example. Just as well, for those extra ships proved invaluable in tackling an immense logistical problem. Not only were ships constantly lost through enemy action, there was also a substantial dilution caused by the need to send ships on the 12,000 mile long route around Africa when the short, Mediterranean route was closed to the Allies. Also, sailings of ships otherwise ready for sea might be delayed while convoys were mustered. Though there was careful planning to sail by shortest routes, the slowest ship dictated the speed of all, and distances were often extended by the need for evasive steering.

To help close the gap, new loading and stowing techniques were developed. Detailed plans of every ship were prepared, so that every inch of cargo space could be identified and loading pre-planned. Thus, small vehicles were loaded inside larger ones; odd corners filled with small items; meat carcasses were boned and concertinaed before loading; and odd-shaped items carried on deck. Even tankers and bulk carriers brought aircraft across the oceans as deck cargo.

A separate pamphlet told of inshore shipping, ***British Coaster 1939–1945*** (CoI/HMSO, 1947), sponsored by the Ministry of Transport. A mystery surrounds its authorship. It is obvious from references in *Merchantmen at War* that both were planned at the same time, and intended to appear in the same year. Why was there an almost three-year gap? One theory is that popular novelist, Leo Walmsley, who revealed in a volume of autobiography that he had been asked to attend at MoI around that time to discuss a writing project, was expected to provide the text. It was a subject that he was well-qualified to write upon, and he was available. However, it is known that he had become disenchanted with authorship, and had other matters to occupy his mind and time. Researchers have tried to discover evidence, but so far without success. Another theory is that Walmsley contracted to provide the text, but put off the task for so long that, eventually, another was persuaded to do it. Whichever it was, the long delay meant that the pamphlet eventually appeared when post-war book-buyers were bored with WW2, so that sales were small, and the pamphlet is now frustratingly difficult to find.

That is a pity, for it has a compelling story to tell. The life of a coastal seaman was very different to that of his deep-sea colleague, who enjoyed at least some respite from threats of air attack. In coastal waters, every voyage was within range of enemy planes, the waters were tricky to sail in, and the influences of wind and tide were greater. Every trip was under constant threat from mines, many by attack from E-boat or submarine and, in some areas, by shells from coastal artillery. The ships tended to be much smaller, with smaller crews, which meant longer hours and less sleep. Navigation in restricted waters meant hours of frenzied activity, perhaps dashing from one wing of the bridge to the other, or up and down ladders and along slippery, sloping decks. The ships had never been built for speed, and many had become old and slow, and prone to breakdown. Younger and fitter seamen generally preferred deep-water ships, leaving the inshore ships to be crewed by older men, and by the very young and inexperienced.

Shorter routes meant that a greater proportion of time was spent manoeuvring in harbours, loading and unloading, highly vulnerable to attack in locations well-known to the enemy, and easily found. Those shorter routes, constricted between shoal waters and defensive minefields were more vulnerable to random minelaying by hit-and-run enemy planes and ships, and the channels had to be swept almost daily to keep them in use. Ships could not enter the channels until routine re-sweeping had been completed. Theirs was an insecure, hectic and hazardous calling.

Also insecure had been the lives of shipbuilders. British shipyards had been badly hit by the pre-war depression, many yards closing and their workforces laid off for years on end. Neglected and badly equipped, the skills of their erstwhile workers eroded, the yards had left apprenticeships uncompleted while younger, more active workers were not recruited. Skilled men had left for other industries, so that the whole infrastructure was in terminal decline. With the approach of war, though, new orders were placed, filling every berth – but what remained of the workforce was disillusioned and embittered, and many had lost the heart and strength needed for heavy manual labour. ***Build the Ships*** (MoI/HMSO, 1946), written by novelist V S Pritchett with Admiralty assistance, was intended primarily to give an account of the war-rejuvenated industry, back on its feet and reorganised for maximum production of new, and rapid repair of damaged, ships. But the darker side of the story was not overlooked.

Now the yards were being modernised and extended, ship designs simplified, skills rejigged so that work could be shared with women and recruits from other industries. Now yards had full order books, and were working round-the-clock, ships were being built faster, with sections prefabricated while awaiting the availability of a berth for assembly. The need to make up, post-war, for the vast numbers of ships lost seemed also to offer hopes for the future.

Yet the saddest part of this compelling story is that Pritchett could warn, as early as 1946, of what could already be seen as the chillingly inevitable serious decline of this successfully revitalised heavy industry. Even when working at its most efficient and productive ever, British ship-building was doomed; no hope could be offered to save the livelihoods of thousands of workers who had rescued their industry and helped to save their nation at a desperate time.

The sites and their rivers would be too small for post-war needs; materials would need to be brought too far; and labour costs would be too high. Even the climate would be wrong! The future for building ships would be against the clock, and that would mean working round-the-clock, bringing prefabricated sections for assembly under cover. The positions, sizes and shapes of British yards would be all wrong, and there would be no room to provide the support services and industries. After the war, building of big ships would increasingly go elsewhere. Britain would have to learn to compete against the quickest and cheapest, building mainly small ships and pleasure craft. Every worker already knew this by 1945, yet continued to give of his or her best while the 'good' times lasted.

Another novelist, Nigel Balchin, was asked to provide the story of aircraft production 1935–1945, which appeared as ***The Aircraft Builders*** (CoI/HMSO, 1947). By the time of its late appearance, its original sponsor, the Ministry of Aircraft Production had been absorbed into the Ministry of Supply, but it was a story worth waiting for: a story of Britain at its best, showing the British genius at its highest and most characteristic. The pre-war aircraft industry had been tiny and fragmented, its output insignificant. The RAF had gone to war with a fighter force that was far too small, and a bomber force both out of date and unsuitable for the job to be done. Despite its losses of planes, it ended the war with a gigantic fleet, modern and capable in every respect.

But it is not sufficient to consider numbers alone, though they are startling – some 120,000 planes were built in Britain during the war. These were made progressively faster, heavier and bigger, while technology leap-frogged itself several times. Though the climb in home-built numbers had been impressive, the surge in quality, performance and capability had been almost beyond comprehension. New methods of construction had been implemented while the numbers employed and locations used multiplied, and factories learned to work around the clock. All that was accomplished in a few short years, and in the face of unremitting attack by the enemy. Before the war was finished, the earlier, almost cottage industry had become the country's greatest industrial force, substantially bigger than both of the next two largest industries combined.

The pamphlet's author had still, in 1947, to be cagey about production statistics and aircraft capabilities, but could reveal some figures. By 1944, for example, one particular manufacturer had increased his plants from one to five, but had multiplied floor area twenty-two-fold. The weight of aircraft delivered (which gives some idea of the technological gain) had increased seventy-fold, though the number of employees had increased 'only' ten-fold! The Spitfire Mk 14 of 1944 was thirty-five per cent heavier than the 1939 Mk 1 but the power output of its engine had been doubled, and the improved power/weight ratio enabled it to fly 100 mph faster. The early options with bombers had been to juggle the three determinants: load, range and speed. In 1939, theoretically any one could be improved at the expense of the other two, the combinations

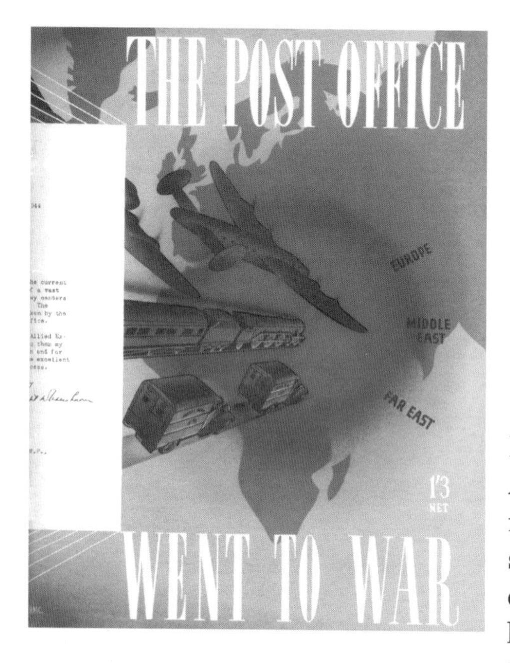

restricted within those parameters. However, 1940's drive and inventiveness soon enabled ranges to be extended, and speeds to be increased, and loads to be doubled. Pre-war, that would have been so far beyond reach for it to have seemed unbelievable that so much could be accomplished in but a few years.

Ian Hay's return from his PR duties in America enabled him to provide two more pamphlets for the series though, sadly, neither did justice either to his own talents or to the achievements of his subjects. The first was ***The Post Office Went to War*** (HMSO, 1946), which the postal and telephone service seems to have commissioned itself, without MoI/CoI involvement. The book is attractively designed, with strong artwork, use of colour on the cover, and packed with interesting photographs, but its text is rather disappointing. The Post Office's varied and important contribution to the war effort deserved better than this.

Reprinted from* Front Line *(MoI/HMSO, 1942)

As well as dealing with the disruption to its normal activities caused by enemy action, and the new responsibilities of forces' mail, with reduced staff it had to provide, adapt and maintain new communications networks for Government and defence services. Extension and repair of these were always top priority, so that staff had to work in front line conditions, often under fire. Many were killed or injured on duty, and after work, the

'Re-lining a 15-inch naval gun. Repair and refitment.'
***Reprinted from* R.O.F. – the story of the Royal Ordnance Factories, 1939–48**
(CoI/HMSO, 1949)

obligations of fire watch, Home Guard and Civil Defence had also to be discharged.

The Post Office was also engaged in secret work, defence manufacturing and communications research. An early task was the desperate need to overcome the communication problems in the tactical use of armoured fighting vehicles. Due to their construction and the noise of their operations, radio communications both inward and outward were severely hampered, and the Post Office Research Establishment was given the urgent task of providing improved radio links and new types of microphones and head-sets. Post Office war-time researchers and engineers were pioneers in many technical breakthroughs – the carrying of hundreds of separate conversations down a single wire is just one example. That, and the other examples cited in the pamphlet may seem in the light of today's knowledge, rather run-of-the-mill, but it should be remembered that these advances were highly significant at the time, and had been achieved largely without the aid of electronics which, now taken so much for granted, were then far beyond science's next frontier.

Ian Hay's next contribution was equally pedestrian, and the resulting pamphlet did not even have the benefit of good design. It must have sold poorly, for it has become so rare that copies are almost never seen today. That was ***R O F – the story of the Royal Ordnance Factories, 1939–48*** (Ministry of Supply & CoI/HMSO, 1949). Again, it is a pity that the story of such a great contribution should be so badly told, and be so difficult to find.

The Royal Ordnance Factories have a very long history – the first was known already to have been in existence in 1560 – and have played a large part in all Britain's wars since at least the 16th century. During WW2, there were three distinct types of factory: manufacturing weapons including shell and bomb cases;

making explosives; and filling ammunition with explosives and fitting fuses. Sometimes, all three might exist on a single, large site, but safety dictated that each should be isolated. The work was demanding and highly dangerous, even without the attention of the Luftwaffe.

The work was also inventive and innovative, carried out to closest tolerances under extreme pressure. The defence of Britain from air attack, for example, depended upon the manufacture of accurate gun barrels, of shells that could be pre-set to explode at precisely the right time and height, and aircraft ammunition that would fire at high speed, under G-forces, without jamming. All were needed in large quantities all around the country, without interruption or delay. Simultaneously, the varied and complex needs of the Navy, and of the Army abroad, had to be provided. All of which called for large numbers of staff – the Chorley Works alone covered 1,000 acres and employed 35,000 workers in 1,500 separate buildings.

But how do you provide both of those mutually-exclusive but essential requirements – large factories, potentially so dangerous that they must be sited far from centres of population, and the large numbers of people to work there that can only be found in those large population centres? The answer is to bring staff from afar, by special trains on newly-laid tracks, provide for three shifts to work around-the-clock, and arrange for all their feeding and welfare needs. A huge operation if undertaken in peacetime, made much harder by black-out, tightest security and constant air raids.

This group of pamphlets, which provides a graphic account of the impressive way in which 'ordinary citizens' of an industrial society faced the challenges of total war, sustaining their efforts through years of uncertainty, danger, hardship and anxiety, should never be allowed to be forgotten. HMSO's record of the people at war still had several more exciting instalments to come.

An important and fascinating story is told by ***Land at War*** (MoI/HMSO, 1945), about British farming 1939–44. This fragile pamphlet in its easily-damaged paper cover is an early work by a writer who later became both popular and highly collectable, Laurie Lee. Thus, its inability to survive careless handling, and its eager pursuit by collectors of Lee's works, mean that it has become both

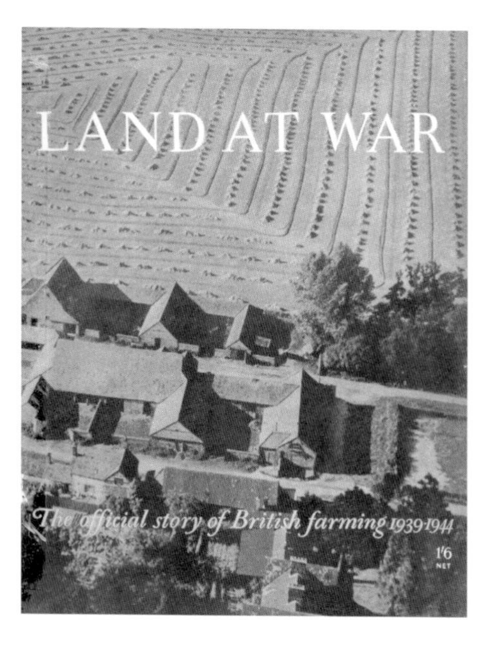

scarce and expensive. Today, a copy in good condition would command a price of £80–£100 in a rare-book shop.

Laurie Lee told this interesting story well, so the pamphlet provides a thoroughly good read. He begins by telling how British farming had been neglected and run down during the inter-war years of cheap, abundant food imports from the Empire. Good farmers and their workers, unable either to justify investment or earn a living, had been driven from the land, while those that remained had often been the lazy, the disinterested, and the incompetent. By 1938, agriculture in Britain was moribund.

The coming of war, and the threat of starvation through U-boat activity changed outlooks overnight. But the land takes longer. It was early foreseen that it would prove impossible to import sufficient animal feeds, and unwise to grow enough at home. That meant that livestock numbers would need to be sharply reduced and maintained at low levels throughout the war, so that fields could be used for growing crops.

That had the effect of creating the illusion of an empty countryside at a time when farming had never been busier, or more productive and efficient. Much more land was brought into production – even wasteland that had not been farmed for centuries, if ever. Increases in the use of machinery enabled reduced numbers of workers to be applied more effectively, further heightening the illusion of emptiness. Under Ministry of Agriculture guidance, farming communities introduced and applied strict systems of supervision and control, to ensure best use of resources, so that production rocketed, and the land was brought back into good heart. Although beyond the scope of Lee's pamphlet, we now know that by the war's end, Britain again had a strong and thriving farming industry. Modernisation was continued into the post-war years so that, until the trauma of the European Union's Common Agricultural Policy began to reverse things again, Britain's farming industry led the world for productivity and efficiency. Lee was able to put this socio-economic background tellingly into a most appealing story of war-time changes in country life and work.

A civilian calling that was over-turned and transformed by war was that of police officer. In ***The Metropolitan Police at War*** (HMSO, 1947), H M Howgrave-Graham, a retired Secretary of London's Police Authority, told how war affected the largest of the country's police forces. The Metropolitan Police (and, presumably, the County Constabularies) had not been so budget-constrained as had the armed forces, and were able to make full and detailed preparations for war. Their efforts had begun as early as the beginning of 1935, and they were ready for Hitler by 3 September 1939.

The nature of police work changed radically though unobtrusively under the Defence Regulations and the Home Secretary's sweeping new powers so that officers became deeply involved in areas of civil life previously firmly closed to them. It is greatly to their credit that their new powers were exercised with enough discretion that most of the population remained unaware that much had changed. In fact, for the war's duration, Britain became almost a 'police state', but without the traditional relationships between 'bobbies on the beat' and citizens being adversely affected. A remarkable achievement!

Although it was not until June 1940 that the first bombs fell in the London area, of the sixty-eight months that the country was at war, for forty-seven months the Capital was more or less under air attack, including intensive periods totalling seventeen months. Reputedly, that was the longest bombardment ever suffered by any city ('And it certainly felt like it,' comments your Author who, apart from three months in Autumn 1944, was present throughout). Police officers were intimately involved with every incident, so that their work was harrowing and exhausting – and without warning could descend into the truly horrific.

The pamphlet includes grim stories that still evoke sympathy for their victims and for those who stood by them. One perhaps less grim, though far from amusing, concerns the man working in his garden who was badly injured by the blast of a bomb that also overturned four beehives. The angry bees, seeking to punish the cause of their discomfort, attacked the casualty, who was too hurt to defend himself. Several rescuers were driven back by the bees, but a

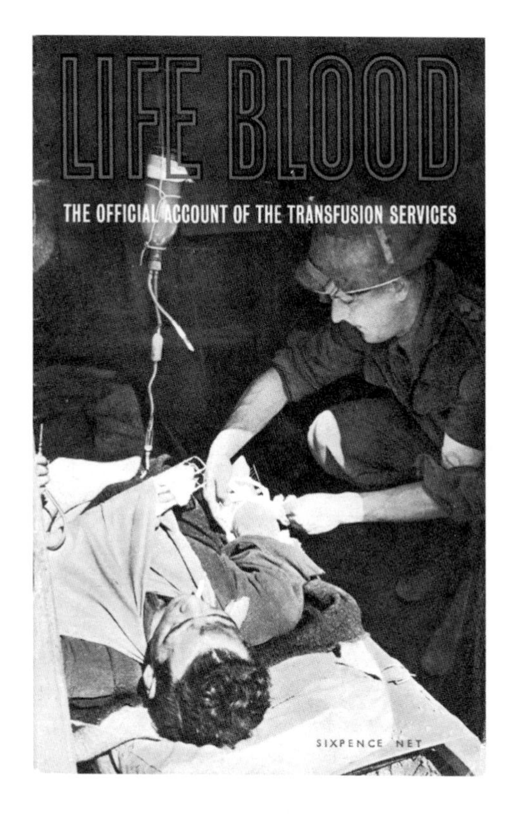

police sergeant persevered, carrying the man to safety, and himself suffering 132 stings in consequence.

Indeed, police officers' bravery and dedication became a byword: almost one hundred Metropolitan officers were awarded the George Cross, the highest civilian bravery award. So thorough had been police preparations for war that, probably uniquely, the service never suffered from under-manning. Indeed, police officers were released to serve in the armed forces, where many were awarded the highest decorations, and quickly rose to senior ranks.

'The Great War' (WW1) had been notorious for the high levels of deaths among the wounded, often caused by delay in battlefield first aid and consequent shock and infection. WW2's record was markedly better, thanks in part to the blood transfusion service, a joint civil-military effort. The trans-fusion service in Britain was begun in 1921 by the Camberwell Division of the Red Cross when four members gave blood for an emergency case, and London Rover Scouts were among the first groups to give blood as a community service. By 1925, serious attempts to organise a service were under way and by 1938, the London Service answered over 6,000 calls for blood. Experiences in Russia and during the Spanish Civil War had proved the need for a comprehensive system.

Expectation of war in 1939 was the trigger for the beginnings of national coverage, and an Army Transfusion Service was set up. The official account is given in ***Life Blood*** (MoI/HMSO, 1945), sponsored by the Ministry of Health. This is the pamphlet that had been begun by Eric Linklater in 1942, but which he had been prevented from finishing (see chapter 3), and it is better for that enforced delay, because it was thus able to tell a more complete story.

By the time of Dunkirk, battlefield transfusions were being given on a large scale, saving many lives and boosting morale. At first, whole blood was usually given, but the service was soon refined to administer blood plasma, which had a longer storage life and revolutionised treatment. Transfusion units routinely accompanied troops into battle where, as well as giving blood or plasma to casualties, they would also collect new blood from colleagues of the wounded – a new interpretation of the soldier's claim to have given his blood for his country! Between 2–30 March 1943, one Field Transfusion Unit operating in forward zones of the North African desert collected 1,776 bottles of blood from troops in the field, and received still larger quantities from base troops. Overall, about one casualty in every six was to receive either blood or plasma, and generally three bottles were needed for each man treated.

'The life-saver.' Reprinted from **Life Blood** ***(MoI/HMSO, 1945)***

Four chief reasons for the vast improvement in survival rates following wounds were new 'miracle' drugs such as penicillin; use of closed plaster treatment for compound fractures; blood transfusion and better organisation of medical services that got casualties to treatment far quicker. Although warfare had become more intensive, and the potential for horrific injuries greatly increased, the rate of deaths from wounds of British and Empire servicemen was reduced to a small fraction of that of WW1.

Those same advances which benefited servicemen also helped civilian casualties, but their numbers at home were far higher than in the earlier war because of the greatly increased level of air attack. Civil Defence services were well supported by voluntary organisations, and significant aid for air raid victims was provided from USA. A truly heart-warming story is told in ***Friends in Need*** (CoI/HMSO, 1947) which, unhappily, is the scarcest of all these HMSO titles, now virtually impossible to find outside specialist reference collections. It is much to be hoped that a modern facsimile

edition (or even a reprint of the original text) may become available, for this is a story which should not be forgotten, of a deep and committed friendship between the peoples of two nations.

The British War Relief Society of America began its work in November 1939, warmly and generously supporting British people at their time of greatest need. It came to be supported by 2 million Americans, who volunteered their time, money and goods, to bring a sustained flood of relief to their beleaguered cousins – mostly through existing British relief organisations, so that recipients were often unaware of the source of the aid and comfort that had been so unstintingly provided.

Among the benefits of this great tide of human kindness that surged across the Atlantic were the equipping of scores of convoy rescue ships (fifty-seven by Autumn 1940 alone) and eighteen motor columns of all needed types of vehicles to bring quick relief to blitzed towns. A lost field hospital was immediately replaced, air-sea rescue floats were stocked, and ambulances were provided to operate nationwide. A particularly impressive feature of the Society's work was the speed of its response to needs, with the seemingly impossible often accomplished almost overnight. The Americans did not wait to be asked for help, but maintained a network of trouble-shooters in Britain, whose job was to identify need and find the quickest way of meeting it. There was no ballyhoo; just fast, hard work. Those wishing to find out more will find it difficult, but Ian Hay's short hardback *America Comes Across* (Hodder & Stoughton, 1942) contains a chapter on the Society's early work, and is well worth seeking out.

Before leaving the Home Front, a brief mention should be made of the Board of Education's ***The Schools in Wartime*** (MoI/HMSO, 1941), one of the earliest pamphlets to appear. It tells how Britain's state education system adapted to wartime conditions, particularly to the disruptions of evacuation, the loss of premises to bombing and requisition, depletion of staff and – most demanding of

Reprinted from* Friends in Need *(CoI/HMSO, 1947)

all – the special needs of children whose fathers were abroad, or whose homes had been destroyed, or who were separated from their mothers and families, perhaps for years. In the midst of unprecedented difficulties and dangers, the schools carried on, with courage and discipline that helped to maintain the stability of national life when it was most needed.

The wide range of HMSO pamphlets are very informative, but are often annoyingly short on statistics. Partly, of course, that was because they were incomplete records, generally covering periods that ended well before the war itself, while both security and morale were limiting factors. However, many of those omissions were made good by a Government White Paper entitled *Statistics Relating to the War Effort of the United Kingdom* published in November 1944. A much shortened digest of that appeared in January 1945 as ***100 Facts About the United Kingdom's War Effort*** (MoI/HMSO, 1945), one of a sub-series of *'100 Facts About ...'* booklets. Because of a self-destruct combination of flimsiness and pocket-size, few examples have survived, unfortunately. This pamphlet is particularly interesting for the early information upon numbers of people mobilised, and their distribution among the Services, war industries and other vital functions, and for the extra dimension it provides on earlier pamphlets in the series.

Far more detailed was ***How Britain Was Fed in Wartime – Food Control 1939-1945*** (Ministry of Food/HMSO, 1946). This makes no gestures towards being a popular account, and requires the reader's undivided attention. But that attention is fully rewarded by a fascinating account of a complex campaign as important as any fought with weapons, the outcome of which was never less than critical. It reveals how the nation's basic minimum requirements were calculated, how and where this food was obtained and distributed, and how changing rations compared with pre-war diets.

The British were fortunate in that they long enjoyed the services of an active and highly competent Minister of Food, Lord Woolton. It was another case of 'the hour producing the man'. Families found the gathering of their food a time-consuming and wearying activity, but the rations always got through. Meals may have been monotonous, and diets depressing, but it remains that the British people entered the war generally undernourished and disadvantaged compared to their opposite numbers in, for example, America or Canada, but emerged from it fitter, leaner and tougher than they had ever been. Wartime diet had been good for their health, which at once began to decline when foods of their choice again became available.

Chapter 6

All Aboard the Bandwagon

The Scramble to be Heard

Edward Hulton, publisher of the hugely popular magazine *Picture Post*, quoted in his editorial in the issue of 28 March 1942, the headline from a recent issue of *World's Press News,* the newspaper industry's own trade paper: 'our stock in Europe is mud to-day!' The reference was to what Hulton described as Britain's 'contemptible propaganda'. *Daily Mirror* correspondent, David Walker, in Lisbon, had written, 'England has become damn near a laughing stock abroad. This is solely due to whatever bunch of pin-wits has been entrusted with explaining the war to the world. The consummate ass who says that we never retire, but only "shorten our lines", who declares that we prefer to have the German battleships at Heligoland, is helping to lose the war for Britain. That noble lord who declared that Britain's aerodromes would be defended with pikes caused a hyena's laugh to ring out right across the Continent. It is equivalent to a military defeat.'

Another correspondent had recently cabled his paper in strong terms at the increasing ineptitude of Britain's official press conferences. A distinguished Swiss journalist had told the world, 'the regular MoI press conferences are mostly a waste of time'. Hulton summed up widespread and virulent press comment with, 'it is quite impossible to feel any confidence whatsoever in Brendan Bracken at the MoI. He is a forceful and witty person who has improved some of the machinery and services of the Ministry, but he refuses to address himself to the fundamental subject of propaganda and the moral leadership of Britain and the cause of decency, freedom and democracy. MoI has been feeble from the beginning ... in the last few months it has lost its reputation for accuracy ... a successor should be found for Bracken without delay'.

All those experienced voices were referring to the daily propaganda output of MoI, and today it is reassuring to read that the Ministry was not much interested in it, and did not trouble to do it well. After all, Goebbels was interested, and did try to do it well (from the Nazi viewpoint), and his was hardly an example to be followed! HMSO's WW2 Paperbacks, though, were another matter. They inhabited only the outer fringes of propaganda. True, they pointed in the same general direction, but they were not written by MoI, but by established authors with public reputations to protect. That part of MoI's output, at least, had proved an undoubted success. Its limitations were recognised and accepted. It was not the pamphlet writers' job to record failures and follies. Their task was to show the real work in hand and chart the paths taken to reach objectives. By doing that – despite, or because of, their selectivity – they uplifted and encouraged with their 'first draft of history' (or propaganda, if you like). The accelerating success of the pamphlets was evidenced both by the widening range of their subjects, and by the many organisations that wanted a slice of the action. Many non-official bodies were also to follow their example (see chapter 7), while more and more Governmental authorities hurried to MoI's doors.

Prominent among these was the new Combined Operations Command, which had secured the services of the doyen of contemporary pamphleteers, Hilary Saunders. He wrote ***Combined Operations*** (MoI/HMSO, 1943), which was to prove yet another worldwide best-seller. The book gave a general account from the forming of the Commandos in June 1940 to the North Africa landings in November 1942, and an introduction to the subject by way of the story of the setting-up of the seminal Combined Operations Development Centre at Portsmouth in 1936.

Saunders' text was frank enough to show the Commandos' 'learning curve' as they sought to inflict a new style of warfare upon a then dominant enemy. It unfolds a story that begins with small and not always successful attacks – 'Red Indian raids' as the Nazis at first sought contemptuously to dismiss them – which rapidly grew in size and power until the book ends with the invasion of North Africa, described at the time as 'a combined operation greatly exceeding in scope and magnitude anything which has been attempted in modern war'.

Later, the world was to learn that printers' proofs of the pamphlet had themselves been used to fool and divert enemy intelligence, by including them as undeniably genuine documents among a case full of spoof papers washed ashore in Spain, attached to a dead body dressed as a Royal Marines major – the famous 'Man Who Never Was'. Such was the impact of Saunders' latest pamphlet, and of its American edition, that it was selected for publication by the American Book of the Month Club – the first time any British Government publication had been accorded such popular distinction. Saunders himself was sent to USA, to travel and lecture widely upon Britain's war effort and aims. On his return, he wrote his *Pioneers! O Pioneers!* (Macmillan, 1944), mainly about his travels and experiences in wartime America, but now particularly valuable for its chapter upon his work as a Government pamphleteer, and the insights he gave upon the philosophy behind the works and the methods used to compile them.

Allied and Commonwealth Governments were sufficiently impressed by the series' purposes and successes to want to join in. The exiled Royal Netherland Government was a particularly staunch advocate of the method, with three pamphlets sponsored, two of them in conjunction with cinema films. Because one of their aims was to record the work of the Dutch Resistance, it was clearly necessary to generalise, even fictionalise, the stories those two were to tell. To do otherwise would have been to condemn thousands to cruel deaths and to set back, if not destroy, the movements they sought to support.

Thus, that ***The Silver Fleet*** (Netherland Government Information Bureau/HMSO, 1943) is but a story written to entertain in no way detracts from its right to be included in this documentary, factual series. The book (by Gordon Wellesley) and the film (written and directed by Wellesley and Vernon Sewell) 'invents' a story of resistance and sabotage, played out by fictional characters, but the Netherland Government ensured that it held up a mirror to real life and told accurately of the dangers faced by loyal Dutchmen in their attempts to resist their oppressors and aid the Allied war effort. It was frank about the existence of Nazi collaborators, and was surprisingly fair to German Occupying Forces. The film is occasionally shown on TV, and both film and book deserve to be taken seriously.

The other pamphlet sponsored by the exiled Royal Netherland Government was ***One of Our Aircraft is Missing*** (HMSO, 1942). The film of the same name (also sometimes shown on TV) had cooperation and advice from the Air Ministry, Admiralty and War Office, and much of the story-line was based upon actual secret information received in London by the Royal Netherland Government. This is by far the more impressive of the two, for it could clearly be seen to be a composite record of individual adventures that everyone knew to be going on, all the time. Written by Emeric Pressburger (author of the then hit, later cult, movie *49th Parallel*) it tells of a Wellington bomber returning from a raid. Its crew bailed out over Holland, to be rescued, helped, and smuggled home by resistance workers. As grim authentification of this admittedly fictionalised account, the Netherland Government Information Bureau included the factual details of five Dutchmen executed in Summer 1941 for assisting in the escape of a British aircrew. That notable film-buff and expert on WW2, Winston Churchill, was loud with his praise for *One of Our Aircraft*, both book and film, which he believed had succeeded superbly in 'telling it how it is'.

The Netherland Government followed with ***Queen Wilhelmina's Navy*** (Netherland Government Information Bureau/HMSO, 1944), written by novelist and military historian David Divine, a wholly factual account of Dutch naval activities in the Allied cause, following the German invasion of Holland in May 1940 to mid-1943. Important units of the Dutch Navy were able to escape their country's surrender to fight on around British coasts; in the Atlantic, Mediterranean and Pacific; and against the Japanese as well as the Germans.

The book itself has a strange history. Commissioned by the Dutch Government, David Divine's text was put into print (though apparently not published), and given the title *The Royal Netherlands Navy*. In that printed form, it looked much like an HMSO-type pamphlet, but bore neither publisher's nor printer's imprints (a legal requirement in UK), and was undated. Under differing titles, the work was apparently published shortly afterwards in both London and New York. Although those two texts differ slightly from one another as well as from Divine's original, all three are substantially the same. Netherland Information Bureau's New York edition used the same cover artwork as HMSO's London edition despite its different title, and there was some variation in internal illustrations and captions. But not enough to make a significant distinction, leaving one to wonder why it was considered worthwhile to make such minor changes.

The Norwegian Government, also in exile, who had participated in MoI's early non-HMSO paperbacks, also sought to come under HMSO's umbrella. Their first was a truly dreadful example of PR at its worst, ***Before We Go Back*** (Royal Norwegian Government Information Office/HMSO, 1944). The book seems, in contrast with others in the series, badly designed and shoddily produced. It relies mainly on poor photographs with unimaginative captions, and the short text does little to fill out the story, reading as though it had been written by a committee with a couple of hours to spare between tasks they regarded as more important. The book did a disservice to the Norwegian people's gallant fight against Nazism, both under the occupation and outside their country.

Fortunately, the balance was more than redressed by the excellent ***Arctic War*** (Royal Norwegian

Government Information Office/HMSO, 1945), which details the roles of free-Norwegian forces and civilians from August 1940 to December 1944, much of their work being secret and lonely, undertaken in a hostile climate and without much support. The book begins with the amazing story of twelve individuals, thrown together by chance in a Salvation Army Hostel in Iceland, who decided to band together to form a 'private army' to fight the whole German nation! In time, they came to occupy large areas of the Arctic, to carry out important raids against the Germans holding Norway, and to provide vital training to British forces, including the newly-raised Commandos. The scope and value of their fight against Nazism, in such inhospitable surroundings, is a saga of courage and endurance.

Denmark, a tiny country on Germany's doorstep, and virtually without defence forces, had been taken over literally overnight by German troops, some brought in clandestinely with the aid of fifth columnists. It, too, had a story of resistance to tell in ***Triumph In Disaster*** (Danish Council in London/HMSO, 1945), by Holger Horsholt Hansen. Most of the information and photographs for the book had been smuggled out of Denmark by patriots, at risk of their lives and under great difficulties. Though the book provides a resumé of resistance against the occupying forces from 1939 to 1944, it concentrates upon one major incident, the defiance of German forces by the largely unarmed and unorganised population of Copenhagen in June 1944.

German occupation, though far from benign, had at least been less savage than in other countries. But then, at a time when they had their hands full elsewhere and could benefit from preserving the status quo within Denmark, their behaviour suddenly reverted to type. Copenhageners might have been content with a species of 'passive resistance' to show their disgust, but the German military quite unnecessarily antagonised them into direct conflict, although they were without enough soldiers to maintain control. The Danes did not have the means to eject the occupiers from their country, but their sudden active resistance diverted German efforts from elsewhere at a time when their forces were desperately needed to stem the Allied advances following D-Day. This spontaneous uprising had the secondary effect of altering the status of Denmark into that of one of the Allies. It heartened resistance to the Nazis in other countries, and inflicted a major psychological defeat upon the enemy at a critical point in the war.

The long hoped-for entry of America into the war, and the arrival of US troops in UK, prompted the appearance of ***Meet the US Army*** (Board of Education/HMSO, 1943). Although the pamphlet could be bought by anyone who wanted a copy, it was not intended for wide general sale but mainly for use in schools. That, and the appearance on the cover of the name of the pamphlet's author, major poet Louis MacNeice, account for its scarcity and high price today. The relatively few copies that have entered the secondhand market have been avidly pursued by collectors of MacNeice's work, driving up the price so that one can expect to be asked £100–£150 for an example in good condition – a remarkable price for a prose work of a mere twenty-four pages.

In view of the book's intention – to disarm prejudices and to inform about a valued ally – it seems strange that it did not appear until July 1943, by which time US troops had been in the country for many months, though perhaps the title's availability was planned for the start of the new school year, in September. It gives a brief commentary upon the advent of the Americans in the European theatre, and provides comparisons of regional differences in USA and UK, and the use of language. The HMSO pamphlet may, perhaps, have been a response to the American military who, from the outset, had taken the trouble to provide their arriving personnel with a guide to explain the British. Though never published by HMSO, it makes an interesting companion to MacNeice's work, and can now be obtained thanks to the initiative of the Bodleian Library, Oxford, who in 1994 published the American text in a sixteen-page pamphlet with the title *Over There*. Not to be outdone, the British Government provided every arriving American serviceman with a free copy of a pamphlet, *Welcome* (HMSO, 1942), not put on general sale, which explained the differences between the two nations that might confuse newcomers to the country.

One early US Government publication to appear over HMSO's imprint (several others were to follow later – see chapter 8) was ***Target: Germany*** (HMSO, 1944), the British edition of the US Army

Air Force's official story of the US 8th Air Force's first year over Europe – although it actually covers the longer period from February 1942 to August 1943. The US heavy bomber fleet, although large and powerful, suffered from the disadvantages that its planes had been designed and built for daylight bombing, and the crews neither trained nor equipped to find their targets by night. By the time 8th Air Force arrived in Britain, RAF Bomber Command had just about overcome those same handicaps, so it was agreed to divide the task: to bomb the enemy around the clock, the Americans by day, the RAF by night. Fortunately, the US bombers were heavily armed and armoured, which helped them to face German fighters.

It is ironic that the US Government felt both justified and proud to tell the story of their airmen's attack upon the enemy, and as early as 1944, while the British Government and its Air Ministry pointedly avoided paying the same compliment to its own heavy bomber force. Indeed, a political and ethical battle of words upon that subject was to rage for years (see chapter 7).

The Australian Government published a record of their Army's service in twenty-eight territories around the world and, when their Commander-in-Chief visited Britain in 1944, he was persuaded by the Imperial General Staff to arrange for its publication in Britain. The resulting pamphlet appeared as ***The Australian Army at War*** (Australian Army Staff/HMSO, 1944), which impresses by showing the diverse contribution made by a nation with a relatively small population, and the vigour and gallantry with which it was delivered. The feeling at the time was that Britons generally, and British forces in particular, had a strong respect and deep affection for their Australian comrades in arms, and would welcome this opportunity both to show that and to learn more about the Australian war effort.

Reprinted from* The Australian Army at War *(HMSO, 1944)

That belief seems to have been justified, for HMSO's pamphlet sold fairly well, judging by the number of copies that can still be found.

That contrasts strangely with the sales of pamphlets dealing with the Indian and Canadian Armies, both of which were also held in high regard by the British. The Indian Army published, in India, a sequence of three books, which appeared there in both hardback and paperback. The first of these, *The Tiger Strikes*, appears to have been later published in Britain by HMSO in hardback only, and may have been the book that the Indian Army Staff had earlier prevented Eric Linklater from writing (see chapter 3). The other two were later published in paperback in Britain. These were ***The Tiger Kills*** (Government of India/HMSO, 1944), which deals with the Indian Divisions in North Africa from June 1941 to May 1943, and ***The Tiger Triumphs*** (Government of India/HMSO, 1946), which carries their story through to the Italian Campaign from Summer 1943 to February 1945.

In accordance with long tradition, Indian Divisions were a mixture of both Indian and British units, and the comradeship, affection and respect that existed between all ranks of the several

nations enjoined played an important part in their great success. *The Tiger Kills*, much longer in the Indian edition than in the scaled-down HMSO version, had been written by two lieutenant-colonels, W G Hingston of the 1st Punjab Regiment and G R Stevens of the Indian Army's Public Relations staff.

The Canadian Army also published at least two paperbacks giving the record of their forces in Europe, but these seem never to have been considered for separate pub-lication in Britain. Instead, part of the Canadian second edition was marketed here by HMSO. Thus, these books cannot be considered as part of HMSO's series but, for the record, they were *The Canadian Army at War: No 1 – The Canadians in Britain 1939–1944*, and *The Canadian Army at War: No 2 – From Pachino to Ortona, the Canadian Campaign in Sicily and Italy, 1943*. The first had been completed by October 1944, compiled and written by the Historical Section of the General Staff, Canadian Military HQ in Britain, but it is not clear from the books themselves quite when they were put on sale in Britain – 1945 or 1946 seems probable for both.

It had been proposed to publish a similar pamphlet that would deal with the Canadian's part in the Normandy landings and operations in Summer 1944, but there is no reference to be found in the later book as to whether it appeared, or went on sale in Britain. The Canadian Army's time in Britain must have been intensely frustrating for the troops, who were held largely inactive as an army of reserve while the country was threatened by invasion, or used as part of the anti-aircraft defence forces. When at last allowed to fight, they went to slaughter or captivity at Dieppe. The Royal Canadian Air Force had played a prominent part in RAF Bomber Command's onslaught upon Germany, and Canadian flyers had also contributed importantly to Fighter Command, alongside squadrons from elsewhere in the Empire and Commonwealth. Those stories seem not to have been told within HMSO's series, but Hilary Saunders wrote *Return at Dawn*, the official story of one New Zealand bomber squadron from June 1939 to July 1942. It was published as a pamphlet in Wellington NZ in 1943, but seems never to have appeared in Britain.

Considerable thought had been given to how liberated or conquered territories were to be administered by the Allies until war finally ended. Possibly with impending Allied Military Governments in Italy and Germany in mind, a record was published of the British Military Administration of territories rescued from the Italian Empire: Eritrea and Somalia. This was ***The First to be Freed*** (MoI/HMSO, 1944), written by K C Gandar Dower, well known before the war as a writer of several books upon Africa, who had also been a pioneer of civil aviation. Sadly, Gandar Dower died before the pamphlet appeared.

It showed how a compassionate victor restored order and vital services, and helped a previously oppressed and disadvantaged population to a better life than had been enjoyed under the Fascists. It would have been both a testament and a reassurance to the exiled governments and leaders of other subjected nations who hourly awaited their turn to be rescued.

The war in the Far East is not well represented in HMSO's series, and blame for that may well fall directly upon Winston Churchill. He was adamant that British attention and efforts should remain focused upon defeating the Germans in Europe, and he had his reasons. He knew that the main burden of beating the Japanese would inevitably fall upon the Americans, and that elements within the US High Command were extremely touchy upon the point. By 1944, Britain was already fully mobilised, there were no more reserves to call upon, and great difficulty was being experienced in maintaining the current effort. The pips were squeaking, and the barrel bottom had been scraped. Also, there were serious political problems – Britain was committed to withdrawal from India, for example – as well as logistical imperatives: there were not going to be enough landing craft for Europe, never mind for the Pacific theatre. The War Cabinet was caught in a vice from which there was no escape.

Only three titles dealing with the Far East were to emerge, and all came very late. First was ***Ocean Front*** (MoI/HMSO, 1945), another in the large-page, magazine format, which relied mainly upon news photos with captions, supplemented by a fairly short text. This provided a perspective difficult to grasp from the other side of the world – the vast size of the battle area. It spread over 5,000 miles from north to south, and 6,500 miles from east to west – far larger than the whole of Europe including Russia to the Urals. It was precisely because the area was too large to defend effectively that the Japanese gains had been made so quickly – the main ones in some ninety days. They had, by then, so over-extended their forces that further conquest was impractical and Allied recovery of lost ground impossible due to lack of resources. Though the USA was itching to revenge itself for Pearl Harbour and the Phillipines, a condition of strategic stalemate had been reached.

The magazine format chosen was ideal for showing how the Japanese reached the limits of their expansion, and how lost territory was recovered, by a remorseless push-back, until the Allies had reached a position from which the invasion of Japan itself could be contemplated. In the event, there was no need to face that last, formidable challenge, although that could not be foreseen in this publication, which takes events only up to November 1944.

Throughout the years of Japan's domination of the islands, a separate, almost self-contained, war had been fought on the mainland, first in a last-ditch defence of India, then by the recovery of Burma against three very different but equally implacable enemies – mountainous jungle, tropical diseases, and the Japanese army. This was described in ***The Campaign in Burma*** (CoI/HMSO, 1946), written for South East Asia Command by Lt-Col Frank Owen (formerly editor of the *Daily Mail*, and the joint author of *The Royal Armoured Corps*, 1945 – see chapter 3). He shows how Allied forces penetrated deeply behind enemy lines, widely throughout Burma, and how they were supplied by air in a country largely without roads or airfields. Large Japanese forces were engaged, and then defeated, both within Burma and by Chinese forces supplied via Burma. Although the USA regarded the Burma campaign as a British side-show, it materially assisted them in their dramatic island-hopping progress across the Pacific.

The story of the earlier Japanese conquest and occupation of some of those islands was told in ***Among Those Present*** (CoI/HMSO, 1946) sponsored by the Colonial Office. Possible defence methods had been considered in 1936, when it had been realised that logistical support would be dependant upon Singapore. But the threat to the islands arose just as Singapore was about to fall, leaving the tiny communities, widely scattered in the vast Pacific, virtually defenceless and undefendable. There were few garrisons, few air strips, few naval patrols. Local administrations had set up their own Home Guard variations, but were almost without weapons and instructors, and most of the locals were simple villagers without exposure to the ways of industrial nations, unfitted to participate in a

'South East Asia Command.' Reprinted from **The Campaign in Burma** ***(CoI/HMSO, 1946)***

'Last ditch.' Reprinted from **The Campaign in Burma** ***(CoI/HMSO, 1946)***

war the nature of which was outside their experience.

Military strategy clearly dictated evacuation of civilians and abandonment of the islands, but hearts and minds revolted at what could only be seen as running away even before the enemy had arrived. The only remaining option was to fight a war from behind the enemy's lines, clandestinely, and with whatever could be improvised. It was to be a long guerrilla war waged by groups of virtually unarmed dozens against a fully-armed and ruthless horde of professional soldiers. It called for unremitting courage and commitment – the supply of which never became exhausted.

This chapter should help to show how the HMSO series did more than just 'inform the people' at home, or provide 'a first draft of history'. The series also had a wider purpose. Many WW2 HMSO Paperbacks titles were translated into other languages and sold around the world, obtaining support for the Allies from the uncommitted, and encouraging those whose countries had been over-run. Some were translated into Russian, to show that Britain was taking hard knocks too, and that there were sound reasons for what Russia regarded as an over-delay in providing relief by opening the Second Front invasion of the European mainland. Selected titles, published in America, at first aided efforts to bring the USA into the war and later demonstrated that Britain and the Empire were continuing to bear their full share of the joint struggle. Thus, the series did much more than just inform the people at home. It also fought a propaganda war abroad, encouraged other combatant nations, and helped to overcome the early isolationist tendencies within America.

Other governments used the series, and copied it, and it had an effect upon the enemy as well. Dr Goebbels both attacked it publicly and privately commended it, holding up individual titles as models for his staff to learn from. That the series attracted such worldwide attention, support and imitation demonstrates, better than could anything else that, by their use of pamphlets, both MoI and HMSO were doing an important job for Britain, doing it well, and helping to win the war.

Chapter 7

The Ones that Got Away

A Private Enterprise War

Evidence that MoI/HMSO's series was never planned as 'a series' is its opportunistic and desultory nature. It leaps back and forth between subjects, without either orderly progression or doctrine of uniform design. So it can hardly surprise that several works which could have fitted seamlessly into HMSO's garment escaped to appear as commercial pamphlets. Little attempt was made to link the publications, and there are startling gaps between those subjects that were covered. Some of those gaps were plugged by non-governmental bodies or by official agencies that did not seek the support of MoI. In some cases, MoI/HMSO had the means to fill the holes in their series, but chose not to do so. Some of the missing subjects had to wait for pamphlet-type treatment until after – sometimes long after – the war.

The coming of peace gave pamphlet writers time to research more widely and compare British with enemy records, and even to write well beyond pamphlet length, so that the particular early quality of 'first draft of history' became harder to achieve – or was deliberately avoided. Some of the non-HMSO pamphlets, though, retained that benefit by being compiled while the events they described had still to be brought to a conclusion, and those deserve to stand alongside the official series, despite their non-official origins.

In contrast, there were some subjects that MoI/HMSO were

prevented from covering, because of their controversial nature or the demands of security. In some cases, political considerations were the primary bar to coverage. Winston Churchill, for example, was firmly against public discussion upon possible post-war changes in the country's social structure, and was annoyed about what he considered to be the premature publication of *The Beveridge Report* (1942), and the resultant intense media coverage and public interest. That is probably the reason why, though the formal report was issued by HMSO, no popular pamphlet upon its content appeared from the same source at the time. (Though at least one did appear a few years later – see chapter 8.)

Security considerations prevented publication of at least one completed manuscript, which had been written at the direct request of a commander-in-chief (*The Night Battle of Britain* – see chapter 2). Long-running squabbles at the highest levels upon the morality and purpose of Bomber Command's strategic bombing of Germany prevented any prospect of an official pamphlet recording the RAF's most conspicuous campaign, carried through with immense bravery by aircrews who endured an appalling casualty rate (see below).

Opportunities overlooked or avoided by MoI were often seized by non-governmental bodies or commercial publishers, so that some scores of such titles appeared. Even if this were the place to do so, it would be impractical to attempt either a full or even representative coverage of them here. It is appropriate, though, at least to provide a flavour of them, particularly where there is a link with HMSO's style and purpose.

An important example dealt with the British Broadcasting Corporation, whose status during MoI's existence was anomalous. Legally, MoI had wartime powers to control broadcasting, but both organisations understood the need to protect the BBC's independence under its Charter, its editorial impartiality, and its authority among listeners both at home and abroad. MoI carefully maintained a 'hands off' policy – occasionally to the annoyance of the Cabinet. The BBC produced and published its own pamphlets; an early effort was ***BBC at War*** (1941), written by Antonia White who, at the time, occupied a lowly and unpleasing post in that organisation, but was later to become an author whose work was collected. As a result, this early booklet has become scarce and expensive. Others were to follow, including a general information pamphlet, ***Calling All Nations*** by T O Beachcroft (1943), and ***London Calling the World*** by Frank Singleton (1945), which dealt with BBC news broadcasts, and in which HMSO did have a hand.

Before the war, the BBC had seemed an aloof and impenetrable organisation, and the wartime need for armed sentries and the examination of passes at its sandbagged doors, could have done little to change that impression. However, behind those guarded doors, it did become much more aware of and responsive to listeners' needs and thereby became an integral part of their lives. The influx of new broadcasters from all walks of life brought a new freshness and vigour, and it went out into the factories, camps and battlefields, to share those perils and discomforts that it reflected. By 1941, the BBC was broadcasting in forty languages to almost every nation in the world as well as informing, encouraging and entertaining the people at home. Its own installations were heavily bombed and many of its staff killed or injured. It was very much an important part of Britain's active war effort.

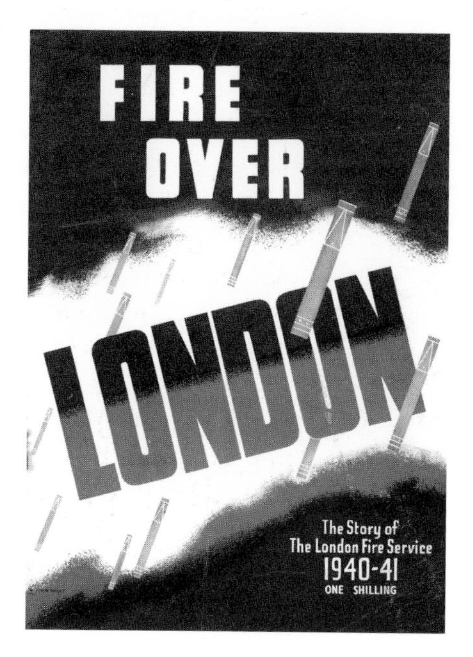

While MoI/HMSO were compiling their comprehensive pamphlet, *Front Line* (1942), which dealt with the work of the Civil Defence organisations nationwide (see chapter 5), the story of London's own Fire Service during the blitz was published as ***Fire Over London*** (1941) by its parent authority, London County Council. Their first major action occurred on 7–8 September 1940, when the London

Brigade had to be supplemented by some 25,000 firemen of the Auxiliary Fire Service, for the great majority of whom that was literally their 'baptism of fire'. In times of peace, a fire needing the attendance of ten pumps had been styled 'a conflagration'. That September night, London had nine fires rating a hundred pumps, nineteen fires rating thirty pumps each, forty fires rating ten pumps and over a thousand smaller blazes.

For the next seventy-six nights (consecutive, excepting only 2 November), German bombers attacked London with high-explosive and fire bombs. The civilian fire service was stretched to its limits, but it responded heroically and never gave in. The Government used this pamphlet record to further its propaganda campaign to bring the USA actively into the war, by arranging for an American edition, titled *Fire Fighters of London in Action*.

Officially-provided services were augmented by many voluntary organisations whose personnel were bound by no obligations other than humanity and their consciences. The British Red Cross Society and the Order of St John of Jerusalem established a Joint War Organisation to ensure that their respective resources were put to best use without overlaps or gaps. A vital part of their work, explained in their pamphlet, ***Prisoner of War*** (1942), was the task of correcting failures of responsibilities by the detaining powers – though even they had to record disappointing lack of concern by the Japanese!

The pamphlet provided the first authentic account of the lives of British prisoners of war in enemy hands; of the efforts made to trace and sustain them; and of work for improvements in their welfare. It included a number of photographs taken in the prison camps, and provided constructive advice for those whose loved-ones were still missing, believed captured. The pamphlet would have been a great comfort and reassurance to many families in Britain.

This was later followed by ***Humanity Keeps an Appointment*** (1944), which gave the Joint War Organisation's further report on support for prisoners of war, but also explained the wider work for civilians and service men and women carried out by the Red Cross and St John. The two civilian services were vital in helping the injured at home and wounded Services personnel in transit, and for the provision of ambulances and nurses. The book also explained the history and organisation of humanitarian services; how money was raised and spent; and how help could be given to advance the work. It was, at last, also able to provide information regarding prisoners of the Japanese, which it had earlier been unable to obtain.

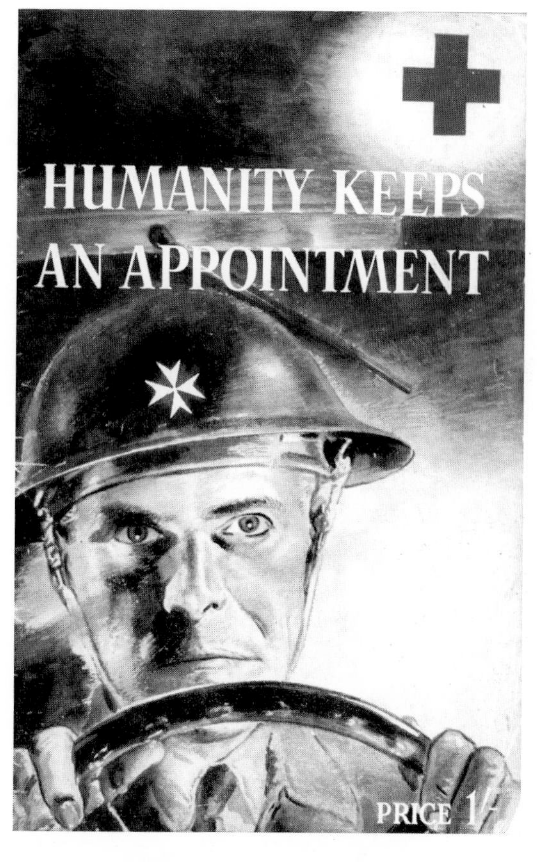

Also closely involved with Government and the Services were the four major railway networks, the nature of whose essential war work might well have alienated all their peacetime customers, both commercial and private. However, although wartime travel by train could be intensely frustrating and uncomfortable, and caused much grumbling, it was widely understood that war needs had to come first, that delays and discomforts must be endured as cheerfully as possible. The companies set up a joint organisation – prophetically called 'British Railways' – and published several pamphlets that helped to explain the problems and dampen down travellers' complaints.

Perhaps the earliest was ***British Railways in Wartime***, which appeared about 1941 and comprised mainly photographs with captions. Later pamphlets, though, were to provide informative texts. These were ***Facts About British Railways in Wartime*** (1943), ***British Railways in Peace and War*** (1944), and ***It Can Now Be Revealed*** (1945). These show that the railways' job was by no means restricted to transport, vital though that primary task was. Through their engineering organisations, they were heavily involved in the actual manufacture or building of planes, landing craft and tanks. Their work for the Services, in both planning and carrying out massive movements of troops and material had been fundamental to the success of some of the war's most important military operations, and both RAF Bomber Command and the US 8th Air Force had been dependant on the railways to sustain their strategic bombing campaign – every '1,000 bomber raid' required thirty-six complete train loads of fuel and bombs to be collected and delivered. A later benefit was that wartime co-operation between the companies considerably speeded the provision of a unified service when the previously competing lines were merged upon nationalisation in 1947.

Although the nation's ship and aircraft builders had to wait until 1946 and 1947, respectively, before their efforts were recorded in HMSO pamphlets, the vehicle builders told their own story much earlier, in ***Drive for Freedom*** (1944). This opens with a surprise: as with so much else in our 'totally unprepared for war' story, in fact the industry's preparations had begun by 1934, when the Royal Army Ordnance Corps began to revive a vast, derelict WW1 munition works, which was to become a depot for the immediate mechanisation of the British Army – a plan that had been formulated as far back as 1928!

The motor vehicles industry and its associated engine builders were to play an enormous part, and not just by the development and provision of an amazing variety of highly-specialised vehicles and their insatiable needs for spares. The industry also made the fire-fighting trailer pumps that saved the country from burning in the blitz, aircraft engines, airplanes and gliders, boats, depth-charges and torpedoes, artillery, machine guns and ammunition, tin hats, and a thousand other necessities.

One industry that could genuinely claim to be fully ready for war was the oil industry. A complete plan, devised in detail from Autumn

1938, was ready to be put into effect, and was applied from 4 September 1939. The separate and competing oil companies entered at once into a voluntary merger, and pooled all their resources to operate for the duration as The Petroleum Board, a civil organisation under Ministry supervision. The pamphlet, ***Petroleum at War*** (1945), a reprint of a series of articles that had appeared in the magazine *The Petroleum Times*, provided the story of British oil distribution in wartime. The Board took over some 18,500 staff operating from 1,100 depots; 5,000 road vehicles; and 10,000 rail tank cars. The decision to switch imports away from South and East coast ports to the West coast (see chapter 5) meant that the Bristol Channel, Mersey and Clyde ports, with only thirty-eight per cent of the handling facilities had immediately to receive a hundred per cent of a rapidly rising total. A 350-mile pipeline circuit, linking distribution depots, was laid, but most of the product had still to be delivered to users by rail and road. In time, the Board was to supply 700 airfields as well as provide for the needs of the Army, Navy and Merchant Service. From start to finish, including the Battle of Britain, the blitz and the D-Day preparations, the Board could fairly boast that never had any RAF or USAAF sortie, or any naval or military movement, been postponed or cancelled for want of fuel or lubricants.

Before leaving civilian activities for those of the armed forces, there is a little mystery to record. Probably about 1941 or 1942, a small-size, forty-page pamphlet appeared, titled ***Eve in Overalls***. It carried the writer's name, Arthur Wauters, but apparently no indication of publisher, price or date! (Remember *The Royal Netherlands Navy*, which had been similarly unattributed at first? See chapter 6.) Because of that, it is difficult to imagine that it could have come from MoI or HMSO, although many of its illustrations do give the impression of being official photographs, and there are similarities between artwork appearing in the pamphlet and artwork in official adverts of that time. Original copies of the pamphlet are now so scarce that, in 1995, the Imperial War Museum, London, published a new edition in facsimile, because of the historical importance of its content.

It deals with many of the new roles taken up by women in wartime, and the way in which their lives had been changed by working in factories, on the land, in transport and communications services, as well as in the forces. Much to the surprise of the chauvinists, wartime conditions enabled women to show that they were superbly good at many of the tasks previously thought to be exclusively male preserves. With minimal training, they were quickly able to operate complex machinery; find and plot approaching aircraft for the gun sites; maintain engines and fit out aircraft. They also proved themselves capable of heavier outdoors work in shipbuilding, farming, and in the fire service, for example. Their work with AA and searchlight batteries, and with the balloon barrage, was invaluable. For women, the war began a programme of social change that was, eventually, to open every occupation to them and, in Education at least, they even achieved equal pay.

In this field of non-official pamphlets, the Services were well represented. HMSO's *The Campaign in Greece and Crete* (1942), at only sixty-four pages, had been relatively short for such an important matter. A distinguishing feature had been the German's use of paratroopers to leapfrog the defenders, and to overcome sea barriers – a particular anxiety in the defence of Britain against invasion. This new development in tactics was more extensively treated in ***Airborne Invasion – The Battle of Crete*** (1944, though actually written in late 1942), by John Hetherington, an Australian war correspondent who was eye-witness to many of the events described. He told a tale, perhaps tactfully exaggerated, of high courage among the smell of inevitable defeat, and of a swaggering, confident retreat, and many of the things he had to say were excised by the censor. The ability of Britain to learn from this unpleasant experience, and to return the compliment, was later covered in HMSO's series in *By Air to Battle* (1945) – see chapter 2.

A gap in HMSO's coverage was filled by the unilateral action of the 15th Army Group, which published its own account of the Po Valley Campaign, which ended the war in Italy – they called their pamphlet ***Finito!*** (1945). It had been a long, hard fight and, as well as beating a determined enemy, something new and remarkable had been demonstrated: a huge force composed of units from many countries, with diverse languages and customs, had fought as an effective and harmonious team, devoted to a single cause. This was 'the United Nations at war' at their best!

A title which certainly ought to have appeared in the series, but did not, was by an earlier contributor, Anthony Cotterell (who had written *Roof Over Britain*, see chapter 3). His ***RAMC*** (1943), a detailed account of the treatment of battlefield casualties, beat HMSO's *Life Blood* (1945) onto the bookstalls. Written to pamphlet length by an Army PR officer, and ideal for the series, somehow it escaped to be commercially published in hard covers by Hutchinson. Also appearing around the same time, but perhaps too hot a political potato for MoI to touch, was another pamphlet-length book in hardcovers, ***The Red Army*** (Cobbett Publishers, late 1943 or early 1944). There was considerable public interest in and respect for the Russian people and their Army, so that the Government felt constrained to walk a very careful line. Every material help must be seen to be given to the ally who was doing so much to beat Hitler, but care had also to be taken that no emotional attachment should be allowed to build which might lead to increasing interest in Communism as a possible route to be followed in post-war Britain. Such a drift might even make Britons reluctant to fight against Russia, should need arise!

It must have been political considerations, too, which were responsible for the slap in the face administered to RAF Bomber Command. After HMSO's two early pamphlets (see chapter 2), *Bomber Command* (1941) and *Bomber Command Continues* (1942), which now serve (admittedly unintentionally) clearly to reveal the RAF 'Heavy Mob's' under-equipped and under-prepared state at the start of war, the Command surely deserved a third, to show how they overcame all those early handicaps, and carried the 'blitz' back to the land from whence it came, turning it upon its inventors. But, when that job had been triumphantly done, elements in the Cabinet and upper levels at the Air Ministry questioned the way in which their directions had been interpreted, and turned their backs upon Sir Arthur 'Bomber' Harris, the man they had charged to carry out their orders. It was a shameful episode.

Two other pamphlets which ought to have appeared from MoI/HMSO, having been specially written for the series, have already been dealt with in chapter 2. These were ***Flying Bombs Over England***, which remained lost until commercially published in 1994 by Froglets of Westerham, and *The Night Battle of Britain* which at the time of writing has still not appeared, although the manuscript, officially approved as a correct record, has been cleared for publication.

There are many other gaps in MoI/HMSO's popular pamphlet series, unaccountably left to commercial publishers to fill after the war. What a fascinating story, for example, would have been a pamphlet record of the build-up to D-Day, its invasion armada, the landings and beach-head battles, if it could have been written and published in 1944! That is not to say that there is no HMSO record at all of those 'missing' activities. There are, indeed, a number of HMSO-published Reports by Commanders, submitted to the Combined Chiefs of Staff, who had them issued in paperback (including one covering the Normandy invasion), but they are necessarily formal in tone, having been written for an entirely different purpose, and are not illustrated. They are all valuable and interesting documents, but they are not within the scope of this book.

Those 'first drafts of history' which escaped HMSO (or were spurned by them) to be published commercially inevitably appeared in a variety of forms, and are now of decidedly mixed value and interest. Many which cried out for pamphlet-type treatment inexplicably appeared in cheap edition hardcovers, while others were dressed up as serious offerings but, even in the darkest days of war, hardly merited a glance from those who wanted to be properly informed. Many were shoddy and opportunistic, or blatantly pushed propaganda and half-truths. Some were superb, and deserve to live for ever.

Demonstrating by contrast how well a short pamphlet could do a big job, and beat a lengthy book hands down, was a curious hardback from Gollancz. Journalist A B Austin had been given a unique chance to study the work of RAF Fighter Command from the inside. When war broke out, he was taken from his job in Fleet Street, and was placed on the staff of RAF Fighter Command's Commander-in-Chief. Told to organise the gathering of news for distribution to the media worldwide, he was given the freedom of Fighter Command, with access to its secrets and the daily battle reports. No doubt he discharged his primary task with skill and dedication. But his subsequent book, *Fighter Command* (Gollancz, 1941) takes two hundred and forty-eight pages to say little more, and sometimes much less, than HMSO's thirty-six page pamphlet, *The Battle of Britain*.

To reinforce the same point, Nicholas Monsarrat, then a serving RNVR officer, wrote three pamphlets: *H M Corvette*, *East Coast Corvette* and *Corvette Command*, first published separately between 1940 and 1943, later collected and re-published as one book titled *Three Corvettes* (Cassell, 1945). These three pamphlets were all written at sea, while the author and his crews were daily engaged with the trials, dangers and adventures of convoy escort work. They were written in parts, at a rush in the intervals between alarms, or when exhausted after action, or as a distraction from hardship, loneliness and fear. As you would expect, they smell of the sea, taste of salt, and are alive in every line. We now know what their early readers could not; that these pamphlets were a prelude to the same author's masterpiece, best-selling post-war novel, *The Cruel Sea*, and a subsequent distinguished literary career.

Another escapee from MoI/HMSO was author Gerald Kersh, who had volunteered to serve as a ranker in the Coldstream Guards shortly after the start of the war. While on leave, he suffered an injury in the bombing, which resulted in his unwilling transfer to non-combatant duties. Because of his fame as a writer and his personal experience in the ranks, he was directed by the War Office to provide a pamphlet on life in the infantry. He spent three months on the project, only to have his manuscript shelved. He decided to convert his efforts into a documentary-style short novel, which appeared as *They Die With Their Boots Clean* (Heinemann, 1941). It became one of the war's biggest selling titles, and probably the best-known of Kersh's many books. Strangely, after War Office's rejection of his factual pamphlet version, his radio adaptation of the novelised version was vetoed by the BBC.

There are rich fields out there, beyond HMSO's pasture, to explore, filled with a challenging mixture of finds that range all the way between the extremes of treasures and dross.

Chapter 8

A Brave New, Cold War World

With VJ-Day in August 1945, and the end of all hostilities, there came to a large degree an end to the need to write 'first drafts of history'. Though the flow of new pamphlets was to continue, the opportunity to research and compare before publishing was now available, while any drive for speed into print had virtually disappeared. Whole new areas of enquiry were opened, upon which it would become important to inform the people. The after-shocks of WW2 would continue to reverberate around the world for many years, with security and censorship continuing to exercise restraints, while the erstwhile valued ally, Russia, had soon to be considered rather as a potential new enemy.

The urge to discuss post-war changes to the social structure of the nation could no longer be denied – and the principal obstacle to doing so (Winston Churchill) was no longer in a position to prevent it. HMSO seized the moment by publishing a series, *Britain Advances*, which generalised about post-war expectations and directions. At home, the people's scepticism about governmental intentions ever to implement the plans set out in the *Beveridge Report* of 1942 could at last be refuted, by quickly clearing a way for the advent of the National Health Service and the Welfare State. On the international stage, the curse of the League of Nations had to be exorcised, so that the wartime alliance, the new peacetime United Nations, could show its determination to continue, post-war, to build a peace that would last.

The UN, the number of its members greatly increased, had first to convert itself from a group of aggressive belligerents into an amalgam of the liberators, the liberated, and the interested onlookers; it had to change into a worldwide peace-seeking and peace-keeping organisation. Its humanitarian task had already begun while the fighting still raged, with the establishment, as early as November 1943, of the UN Relief and Rehabilitation Administration (UNRRA). It had been quickly into print, in Britain, with the pamphlet, ***Helping the People to Help Themselves*** (UN Information Organisation/HMSO, June 1944), which described how and why UNRRA had been set up and the machinery adopted to achieve its aim of meeting the urgent needs of newly-liberated countries. Its task was historically unprecedented – quickly to relieve 500 million Axis victims, worldwide, of hunger, disease and malnutrition.

UNRRA's immediate job was to gather food, seeds, farm machinery, medical supplies and fuel from around the world, and get them to the liberated countries of Europe in the fastest possible time. These vital supplies then had to be distributed throughout war-torn countries whose transport systems had been devastated. At the same time, UNRRA had to accomplish the stupendous task of repatriating some twenty to thirty million prisoners, hostages, refugees and enslaved workers, needed back home but often too desperately sick or enfeebled to look after themselves. One example of the magnitude of this problem – just transport alone to return the 1.8 million Frenchmen in Germany would require one train every hour, around the clock, non-stop for three months. In the meantime, they had to be found, gathered, fed and housed, and home-coming reception arrangements made. A similar problem of greater magnitude would then have to be dealt with in the Far East.

Another pamphlet soon followed, ***The United Nations Today and Tomorrow*** (UN Information Organisation/HMSO, 1945), which provided a commendably clear explanation of a difficult subject, the birth of the UN in January 1942, when twenty-six nations signed its declaration; the development of the wartime organisation; its original combatant role; and its conversion into a means to co-ordinate the rebuilding of a shattered world. By June 1944, the UN team had expanded to forty-five nations. By the war's end, the member-nations of the UN represented some 1,500 million people, nearly three-quarters of the world's then population – the greatest team that had ever been assembled in the history of mankind.

The UN Information Organisation that published those two pamphlets, incidentally, was the successor to the earlier Inter-Allied Information Committee, based in London, which had published a sequence of eight small reports between March 1942 and August 1944, which had dealt with conditions in Axis-occupied territories. These had covered such subjects as persecution of the Jews and of other religions; the Fascist systems of hostages; slave labour and deportation; rationing and the oppression of education. Truly, a world turned upside-down. A small world, too, for the Chairman of that Inter-Allied Information Committee was none other than Arthur Wauters, whom we met in the previous chapter as author of *Eve in Overalls*. Wauters had been the official delegate of the Belgian Government to Britain's MoI and, towards the war's end, was to provide HMSO with the text for their pamphlet, *Britain's Social Services Today and Tomorrow*.

Graphic examples of the shattered state of large parts of the world, if any were needed, were the two Japanese cities, Hiroshima and Nagasaki. There does not seem to have been any 'popular' official pamphlet upon the atomic bombs attack in August 1945, but a British Mission had been sent to Japan that November, with instructions to report to the Chiefs of Staff. Their task was to arrive at general conclusions on the effects to be expected should similar bombs fall elsewhere. Britain would not be caught wrong-footed next time – planning for WW3 was already in hand! The Committee's response was published as ***The Effects of the Atomic Bombs at Hiroshima and Nagasaki*** (HMSO/Home Office and Air Ministry, 1946). Although the report told of what had been seen in Japan, and what could be learned there, its intention was clearly spelled out as what should be expected were atomic bombs to fall on cities that its readers knew well. For the British reader, a spine-chilling effect is provided by the Report's comparisons: the population of Hull closely matched that of Hiroshima, while that of Portsmouth matched Nagasaki – two English towns that had been particularly badly blitzed by the Germans.

This, and many of the other pamphlets dealt with in this chapter, are entirely different in appearance, tone and intention from most of those which had appeared earlier. They are more formal in their presentation of text, less well illustrated or even not illustrated at all, and rather dour and official-looking, externally. With a few exceptions, it seems that no need was felt to address a mass audience in a popular, easy-read, format. The day of the block-busting best-seller was clearly seen to be over! Indeed, some of the pamphlets directed themselves towards an extremely limited readership, and probably never went on general sale at all. As a result, they are now very seldom seen.

In Germany and Italy, though the devastation was lesser in degree than in the two small Japanese cities, it was nonetheless severe and much more widespread. An unusual aspect of the consequences of that was highlighted by the publication of several reports in pamphlet-form dealing with the losses and survivals of works of art. As with the Report of the British Mission to Japan, these rather specialised works cannot be considered as 'popular' pamphlets, and are certainly not similar in either intention or tone to those that appeared during the war years, but they do show how concern had switched from finding out how the war was being won to learning to clear up the mess and begin again.

In fact, the War Office had been very quickly off the mark, assessing what had been lost and what saved in Sicily, almost before the smoke of battle had cleared. As the Allied armies moved up the leg of Italy, they continued the process, rapidly, area by area, as soon as possible transferring responsibility to Italian officials. A detailed report upon Southern Italy was ready for publication even before Northern Italy had been taken! In fairly short order, surveys of survivals and losses, and reports on the preservation and restitution, of works of art, archives, etc., were published by HMSO on Southern Italy, Northern Italy, British Zone of Germany, Greece, Austria and unoccupied, but nonetheless heavily damaged, Malta.

All of that work, and of the steps taken in other areas by British forces, was summarised in a pamphlet which, though admittedly of specialised interest, came nearer to the 'popular' concept. That was published with the accurate but unwieldy title, ***A Record of the Work Done by the Military Authorities for the Protection of the Treasures of Art and History in War Areas*** (HMSO/War Office Civil Affairs, 1947), compiled by Lt-Col Sir

Leonard Woolley, who had been the War Office's Archaeological Adviser. This pamphlet even includes a chapter on work done in London.

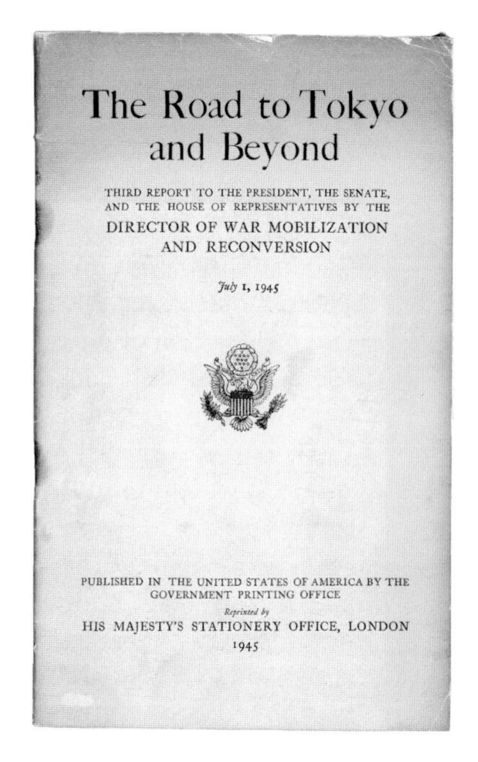
The Road to Tokyo and Beyond

THIRD REPORT TO THE PRESIDENT, THE SENATE, AND THE HOUSE OF REPRESENTATIVES BY THE DIRECTOR OF WAR MOBILIZATION AND RECONVERSION

July 1, 1945

PUBLISHED IN THE UNITED STATES OF AMERICA BY THE GOVERNMENT PRINTING OFFICE

Reprinted by

HIS MAJESTY'S STATIONERY OFFICE, LONDON

1945

Consideration of how to end the war, and how to handle the problems that would inevitably follow, were revealed in the somewhat cryptically named ***The Road to Tokyo and Beyond*** (a US Government publication reprinted in pamphlet form in Great Britain by HMSO, 1945). The Report upon which it was based had been completed before the atomic bombs had been dropped, and its authors had not been party to that plan. Accordingly, the pamphlet opened by envisaging what might have been – a gigantic campaign to push the Japanese forces back to their homeland, and to invade. Such an undertaking would have been the biggest movement of men and material ever put in hand; would have included the transfer of three million troops from Europe halfway around the world; and would have brought Allied personnel in the combat zone to almost six million. The casualties would have been enormous. It is salutary to realise that such plans were actually being made, and that, had they been required to have been carried out, the initial movement and continuing maintenance strains upon resources would have been unprecedented, their consequences long-lasting. In the event, the end was achieved by different means. The main body of the pamphlet dealt with the future conversion of nations' economies from war to peace, looking at the whole world but using the US as an example. The scale of the needed changes, and their far-reaching effects, spelled out here, are still mind-boggling!

At last, previously secret information could begin to be released – though still only sparingly and with caution, for the Russians were watching, and making notes. Two further US Government Reports reprinted as pamphlets in Britain by HMSO should be mentioned.

First was ***Radar – A Report on Science at War*** (1945), which admitted that the enemy, too, had been enjoying its benefits, and revealed that its use had, more than any single development since the aeroplane, changed the face of warfare for ever. Amongst other things, it had taken the reliance upon luck out of both anti-aircraft defence and bombing, and had enabled full-scale naval battles to be fought out without anyone involved on either side seeing the opposing forces.

The pamphlet also had something to say about the effects of radar upon the post-war world, correctly forecasting both the improvements it would offer for travel by air and sea, and its role in the birth of a major new, world-wide industry – electronics – that would have profound and far-reaching effects on the shape of our daily lives. The second pamphlet also dealt with a new force that would change lives, ***Atomic Energy*** (1945), but did not look towards the future – if any! Instead, it gave a general account of the development of methods of using atomic energy for military purposes – a history of work in the USA since 1939. To emphasise that this was in no sense a 'popular' pamphlet account, it states that 'the average citizen cannot be expected to understand how an atomic bomb is constructed or how it works'. The pamphlet also issued the warning that all the information that could be released without endangering national security would be found therein, and it was no use anyone – Press or scientists – applying for more, for they would not get it!

It seems likely that the publication in Britain of those two US works might have been largely responsible for a debate that resulted, in due course, in the appearance of a genuinely 'popular' style pamphlet (in fact, a substantial paperback) nearer to the traditional mould, ***Science at War*** (Department of Scientific and Industrial Research/HMSO, 1947). This also dealt with radar and the atomic bomb, but in an easily understandable way, and provided fascinating additional chapters upon how Operational Research had changed methods of fighting, and how scientific discoveries and developments had transformed war at sea. Its joint authors, J G Crowther and Professor R Whiddington, succeeded in explaining difficult issues for the non-scientific reader.

The book also explains how the development of Operational Research became one of the chief scientific features of WW2, with science entering into warfare to a wholly new degree. Hitherto, its role had mainly been as a source of ideas for new weapons and methods of improving old ones. In WW2, though, scientific method was applied more consistently and deliberately to the ways in which weapons were used and to the conduct of military operations. Analysis had been able to predict, for example, an optimum size for convoys, so that efficiency rose sharply, with the percentage of losses significantly reduced by increasing the number of merchant ships while the number of escorts could remain unchanged. Analysis had also overturned previous criteria for aircraft maintenance, eventually providing a one hundred per cent increase in operational flying hours without increase either in the number of planes or ground resources. Although the book was published too early to be able to say so, it can now be seen from information it provided in 1947 that the type of domestic outdoor TV aerial most commonly seen today is, in fact, a peaceful development from failed Japanese experiments to invent a 'death ray'!

Two enjoyable examples of the ways in which scientists and the Services could combine to provide non-destructive techniques were revealed in two post-war pamphlets. The earlier, which celebrated the 150th anniversary of the Admiralty's Hydrographic Department, ***Charting the Seas in Peace and War*** (HMSO, 1947), explained how much Britain's Navy had contributed to the safety and well-being of the world's seafarers. British marine surveying began seriously from about 1750 and (recurring bouts of Treasury parsimony permitting) had established a continuity of devotion, endurance and inventiveness which had been made available to the world. However, wartime development of faster vessels of increasing draught meant that the surveyors could never regard their task as finished, and by the end of WW2 the greater part of the coastal waters of the globe were again overdue for resurvey. Fortunately, wartime-improved equipment would enable that massive job to be done quicker and more accurately than ever before.

This was followed by ***War and Archaeology in Britain*** (Ministry of Works/HMSO, 1949). Many previously unsuspected ancient sites were revealed by wartime construction of facilities, or by bombing, while many already-preserved monuments were damaged and needed to be protected for the future. The Ministry of Works was active throughout the war in these respects, as well as in the actual removal to safety of other buildings. Newly discovered sites could not be excavated and fully examined at the time, but adequate care was taken either to record evidence or re-plan building works, to allow for proper investigation when peace returned. As a result, post-war archaeologists found themselves with an enormous backlog of pending work, sufficient to last for decades! It is comforting to learn that, even in the darkest days of the war, with invasion hourly threatened and the army at home virtually unarmed, thought and attention was given to advancing our knowledge of our forefathers and preserving the distant past for coming generations. Civilisation could still see beyond the barbarian at its gate.

Those who had been fortunate to survive the war still had another ordeal to endure. The bleakness and austerity of the early post-war years will never be forgotten by those who lived through them. Though the people of Britain were, of course, far better off than those of battle-shattered Europe, nonetheless they hardly lived the lives of victors. Food and clothing remained strictly and straitly rationed, weekly allowances often reduced below wartime levels, while furniture and housing were desperately short and of poor quality if at last obtained. There seemed to be perpetual crises with fuels, foreign exchange and imports. Townscapes were drab, bomb damage unrepaired and travel was a miserable ordeal. Bread, never scarce during the war years, was put on ration. Most of home production had to go for export, and much food that could have been obtained for British tables had to be diverted for the starving millions in Europe.

The former ally, Russia, seemed to have adopted the role of implacable opponent, and had acquired an empire that, by threatening the future of peace, slowed further the painfully gradual return of prosperity and plenty. The Iron Curtain was impenetrable even by goodwill and diplomacy, and the Cold War had become bitter.

The Communist bloc had emerged as a nuclear power, and continued to maintain enormous and constantly threatening military forces. World War Three seemed always to be just over the horizon and, like Hitler's promised invasion in 1940, almost daily expected.

There could be no doubt that Britain still needed its RAF. Its vital work was described in detail in a pamphlet that reported upon a new crisis, ***Berlin Airlift*** (Air Ministry/CoI, 1949) an account of the British contribution, written by Dudley Barker, who had served in Hilary Saunders' old department at the Air Ministry. It was alarming to learn that the RAF, only so recently a dominating force, had been so quickly reduced by economies as to be able only to take responsibility for a fraction of the effort needed to sustain part of a single city, and had insufficient resources even for that, needing to sub-contract part of its role to civil airplanes and crews. Air and ground crews worked around the clock, stretched to the limit, for months. Demobilisation of servicemen had to be delayed, reserves put on stand-by, and conscription of young men tightened. Eventually, the Russian threat was faced down, and the people of the Allied zones of Berlin were rescued from the threats of cold and hunger, and the risk of absorption into the Communist bloc.

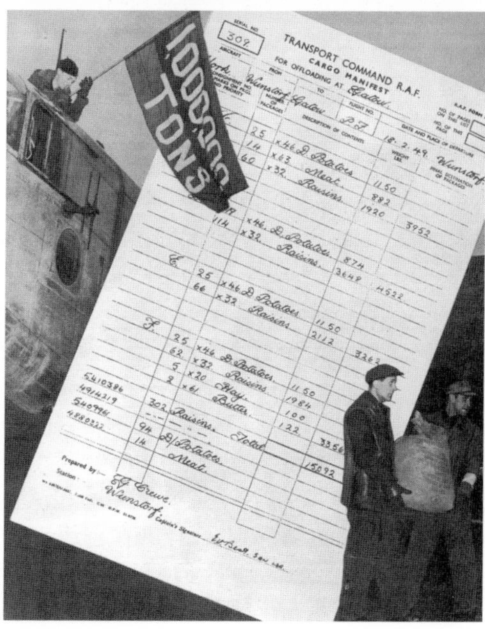

'Lots were drawn for the honour of carrying the airlift's millionth ton on February 19th. The RAF won.'
***Reprinted from* Berlin Airlift**
(Air Ministry/CoI, 1949)

Perhaps the pressures of coping with the Berlin Airlift caused a re-think about the peacetime role of the RAF, and re-engaged the minds of politicians and the defence ministries. A further pamphlet was to emerge, ***A Future In It*** (Air Ministry/HMSO, 1950), the story of the men and women who were carrying on the traditions of 'the few'. Its author is not revealed, but was described as an outsider, chosen because he had served in the wartime RAF, a civilian allowed to return to the service for a short time, to discover what its post-war life was like, and to describe it for a new generation of volunteers and conscripted men.

Rather like the earlier *The Navy and the Y Scheme* (1944), it gave a snapshot of Service life, but it described a Service very different from that of the war years. This was an air force of jet propulsion, early warning systems, electronics, supersonic flight, of short service commissions and university degrees – and of nuclear bombs and missiles. The RAF was depicted as an exciting, up-to-the-minute, technical environment, an important and challenging career that would fit the recruit for an eventual highly-paid return to civvy street.

All that technology was soon to be put to the test, in earnest. We know now that the ultimate challenge from the Communist bloc did not emerge, and that WW3 was at least postponed for the lifetimes of those who had lived through WW2. However, the chances of that did not seem great at the time, and they seemed particularly bleak in Summer 1950, when the North Korean Army crossed the 38th parallel to invade South Korea. Here was a test for the resolution and courage of the United Nations. The Security Council quickly adopted an American Resolution and recommended all UN Members to send assistance to the latest victim of aggression – in exhilarating contrast to the cowardice and indecision of the old League of Nations.

The story of the Commonwealth's part in the Korean Campaign, from the outbreak of war until the end of July 1951, was told for the Admiralty, War Office and Air Ministry, in ***Our Men in Korea*** (CoI/HMSO, 1952) – now surprisingly hard to find despite a print run of 20,000 copies. It marked the return of an old friend, Eric Linklater, who was chosen to visit Korea and to write the book. Thus, Linklater has the distinction of providing some of both the earliest and latest pamphlets in HMSO's series. The war in Korea was a terrible one, lasting from June 1950 until July 1953, with intense fighting ranging back and forth, literally over the whole country. Early North Korean gains were quickly lost to a determined UN push-back which, in turn, prompted the Chinese to intervene dramatically. After much death and destruction, and appalling cruelties (two George Crosses and one George Medal were awarded for the sustained valour of prisoners of war), a stalemate was eventually achieved, with the protagonists glaring at one another with implacable hostility across the so-called 'peace line' for several decades. Almost a thousand British Services personnel had been taken prisoner and, in 1955, the Ministry of Defence published an HMSO booklet, *Treatment of British Prisoners of War in Korea*, which described their suffering and detailed the harsh and inhuman conditions of their captivity.

In the same year that *Our Men in Korea* was published, there also appeared ***Malaya: The Facts Behind the Fighting*** (CoI and Colonial Office/HMSO, 1952). That can hardly be considered as in any way related to WW2, and has been included here only to show that the successful pamphlet formula continued to be used to inform the people well after that war's conclusion. Although rather short (only twenty-four pages including its cover), the pamphlet is strongly reminiscent of the output between 1941 and 1945, and it presents the details of the forces' armed struggle with Communist terrorists in a similar manner to their WW2 campaigns.

This pamphlet marks the end of our examination of HMSO's series and its offshoots, which had started quietly in 1939, gathered momentum to flourish during the period 1941–1947, and then dwindled, finally to end in 1952. Thus, for some fourteen years, HMSO's series informed the people upon the cataclysmic upheavals represented by WW2 and its after-shocks. After the series' demise, Governments continued to inform the people, but new methods had become available with the re-opening of the television service, its gradual extension, and a return to publishing procedures at last freed from censorship and paper shortages.

The need for a 'first draft of history' had been overtaken by the return of time and resources to tell the story of Britain in WW2 at length and in detail. There is no doubt that the post-war public was war-weary, beset by unexpected, seemingly intractable problems of peace-time, and more interested in its immediate future, always assuming that it had one which, thanks to frequent heightenings of Cold War tensions, often seemed doubtful. The years of post-war austerity were dreary beyond belief, and the prospects of Britain weathering its recurrent international financial crises often looked bleak. The later titles in HMSO's series sold in ever-diminishing quantities. Those last few have become so hard to find today as to be almost forgotten, even by the generation that lived through Britain's 'finest hour'. To their children, and grandchildren, HMSO's record of that past has become another country. Even so, it remains well worth a visit.

It would be rash to claim that all relevant titles have been covered in this book, for it remains likely, to say the least, that others will emerge from the shadowy corners of forgotten collections and dusty second-hand bookshops, to seek admittance to the ranks. Many, though, do still remain in abundance, fifty and more years after first publication, reflecting the early strength and the endurance of the series, as well as the best-selling nature of some of its titles. Others, unhappily, have almost disappeared, to be found only with difficulty after long searches. Yet others, a few, really have been lost, so that even extended hunting and enquiry fails to disclose a single copy.

Happily, there is a movement to reintroduce these with modern reprints, usually in facsimile, which give an authentic wartime flavour to these replacements.

Thus, those who might wish now to build only a representative collection can do so without either much difficulty or expense. Thirty or forty titles could be assembled quickly and cheaply with but little effort. However, it will be a different story for anyone who aspires to a complete – or even nearly complete – collection. That will require dedication of effort, much time and a noticeable expense. The chase will be enjoyable, though, and the reward worthwhile. If new titles, not covered here, are found, the author would certainly like to hear about them. Good hunting!

Printed in the United Kingdom for HMSO Dd 302082 C15 9/96

WW2 HMSO Paperbacks, and non-HMSO titles, covered in the text

---

Chapter 1

National Service, HMSO, 1939
How Hitler Made War, MoI/HMSO, 1939
The Assurance of Victory, MoI/HMSO, 1939
The Battle of the River Plate, HMSO, 1940

Chapter 2

The Battle of Britain, MoI/HMSO, 1941, for Air Ministry
Bomber Command, MoI/HMSO, 1941, for Air Ministry
Air-Sea Rescue, MoI/HMSO, 1942, for Air Ministry
Bomber Command Continues, MoI/HMSO, 1942, for Air Ministry
Coastal Command, MoI/HMSO, 1942, for Air Ministry
One of Our Aircraft is Missing, HMSO, 1942 (see also chapter 6)
We Speak from the Air, MoI/HMSO, 1942, for Air Ministry
Over to You, MoI/HMSO, 1943, for Air Ministry
The Air Battle of Malta, MoI/HMSO, 1944, for Air Ministry
There's Freedom in the Air, MoI/HMSO, 1944, for Air Ministry
Atlantic Bridge, MoI/HMSO, 1945, for Air Ministry
RAF Middle East, MoI/HMSO, 1945, for Air Ministry
By Air to Battle, MoI/HMSO, 1945, for Air Ministry (see also chapter 3)
Merchant Airmen, CoI/HMSO, 1946, for Air Ministry
The Battle of the Atlantic, CoI/HMSO, 1946, for Admiralty and Air Ministry (see also chapter 4)
Flying Bombs Over England, Froglets Publications, 1994

Chapter 3

The Northern Garrisons, MoI/HMSO, 1941, for War Office
The Battle of Flanders, HMSO, 1941, for War Office
The Defence of Calais, MoI/HMSO, 1941, for War Office
The Destruction of an Army, MoI/HMSO, 1942, for War Office
The Abyssinian Campaigns, MoI/HMSO, 1942, for War Office
The Campaign in Greece and Crete, MoI/HMSO, 1942, for War Office
The Highland Division, MoI/HMSO, 1942, for War Office
They Sought Out Rommel, MoI/HMSO, 1942, for War Office

The Battle of Egypt, MoI/HMSO, 1943, for War Office
Roof Over Britain, MoI/HMSO, 1943, for War Office and Air Ministry
The Eighth Army, MoI/HMSO, 1944, for War Office
Tunisia, MoI/HMSO, 1944, for War Office
The Royal Armoured Corps, HMSO, 1945, for War Office

Chapter 4
Ark Royal, MoI/HMSO, 1942, for Admiralty
East of Malta, West of Suez, MoI/HMSO, 1943, for Admiralty
Fleet Air Arm, MoI/HMSO, 1943, for Admiralty
His Majesty's Minesweepers, MoI/HMSO, 1943, for Admiralty
The Mediterranean Fleet, MoI/HMSO, 1944, for Admiralty
The Navy and the Y Scheme, HMSO, 1944, for Admiralty
The Royal Marines, MoI/HMSO, 1944, for Admiralty
His Majesty's Submarines, MoI/HMSO, 1945, for Admiralty
The Battle of the Atlantic, CoI/HMSO, 1946, for Admiralty and Air Ministry

Chapter 5
The Schools in Wartime, MoI/HMSO, 1941, for Board of Education
Front Line, MoI/HMSO, 1942, for Ministry of Home Security
The Saga of San Demetrio, MoI/HMSO, 1942, for Ministry of War Transport
Transport Goes to War, MoI/HMSO, 1942, for Ministry of War Transport
Manpower, MoI/HMSO, 1944, for Ministry of Labour & National Service
Merchantmen at War, MoI/HMSO, 1944, for Ministry of War Transport
Land at War, MoI/HMSO, 1945
Life Blood, MoI/HMSO, 1945, for Ministry of Health
100 Facts About the United Kingdom's War Effort, MoI/HMSO, 1945
The Post Office Went to War, HMSO, 1946
How Britain Was Fed in Wartime, HMSO, 1946, for Ministry of Food
Build the Ships, MoI/HMSO, 1946, with Admiralty approval
The Metropolitan Police at War, HMSO, 1947
The Aircraft Builders, CoI/HMSO, 1947, for Ministry of Aircraft Production
British Coaster, CoI/HMSO, 1947, for Ministry of Transport

Friends in Need, CoI/HMSO, 1947
R.O.F. - The Story of the Royal Ordnance Factories, CoI/HMSO, 1949 (Ministry of Supply)

Chapter 6
One of Our Aircraft is Missing, HMSO, 1942, for Netherlands Government Information Bureau
Combined Operations, MoI/HMSO, 1943, for Combined Operations Command
The Silver Fleet, HMSO, 1943, for Netherlands Government Information Bureau
Meet the US Army, HMSO, 1943, for Board of Education
Queen Wilhelmina's Navy, HMSO, 1944, for Netherlands Government Information Bureau
Before We Go Back, HMSO, 1944, for Royal Norwegian Government Information Office
Target: Germany, HMSO, 1944 (reprint of a US Government publication)
The Australian Army at War, HMSO, 1944, for Australian Army Staff
The First to be Freed, MoI/HMSO, 1944
The Tiger Kills, HMSO, 1944, for the Government of India
Arctic War, HMSO, 1945, for Royal Norwegian Government Information Office
Triumph In Disaster, HMSO, 1945, for Danish Council in London
Ocean Front, MoI/HMSO, 1945
The Canadian Army at War, published in Canada, as two paperbacks, in 1945 and 1946, sold in UK by HMSO
The Tiger Triumphs, HMSO, 1946, for the Government of India
The Campaign in Burma, CoI/HMSO, 1946, for S E Asia Command
Among Those Present, CoI/HMSO, 1947, for the Colonial Office

Chapter 7
BBC at War, 1941, BBC
Fire Over London, 1941, Hutchinson for London County Council
Prisoner of War, 1942, Horace Marshall for Red Cross & St John
Eve in Overalls, publisher/date uncertain, possibly 1941 or 1942
British Railways in Wartime, ?1941, British Railways Press Office
Calling All Nations, 1943, British Broadcasting Corporation
Facts About British Railways in Wartime, 1943, British Railways

Press Office
RAMC, 1943, Hutchinson
The Red Army, 1943 or 1944, Cobbett Publishing
British Railways in Peace and War, 1944, British Railways Press Office
Humanity Keeps an Appointment, 1944, Horace Marshall for Red Cross & St John
Airborne Invasion, 1944, R Schindler, Cairo
Drive For Freedom, 1944, Hodder & Stoughton for the Society of Motor Manufacturers & Traders
It Can Now Be Revealed, 1945, British Railways Press Office
Finito!, 1945, HQ 15th Army Group, Italy
London Calling the World, 1945, BBC/HMSO
Petroleum at War, 1945, The Petroleum Times
Three Corvettes, 1945, Cassell, collecting three pamphlets – *'HM Corvette'*, *'East Coast Corvette'* and *'Corvette Command'* – originally published separately, 1940–1943

Chapter 8
Helping the People to Help Themselves (UNRRA), 1944, HMSO/United Nations Information Organisation
The United Nations Today & Tomorrow, 1945, HMSO/United Nations Information Organisation
Works of Art in Italy, Losses and Survivals in the War, 1945, HMSO/War Office (and similar publications dealing with Germany, Greece, Austria and Malta) 1946
Radar - A Report on Science at War, 1945, HMSO/US Government
The Road to Tokyo and Beyond, 1945, HMSO/US Government
Atomic Energy, 1945, HMSO/US Government
The Effects of the Atomic Bombs at Hiroshima and Nagasaki, 1946, HMSO/Home Office & Air Ministry
Charting the Seas in Peace and War, 1947, HMSO/Admiralty
Science at War, 1947, HMSO/Dept of Scientific & Ind'l Research
The Protection of the Treasures of Art and History in War Areas, 1947, HMSO/War Office Civil Affairs Branch
War and Archaeology in Britain, 1949, HMSO/Ministry of Works
Berlin Airlift, 1949, CoI/HMSO/Air Ministry
A Future In It, 1950, CoI/HMSO/Air Ministry
Our Men in Korea, CoI/HMSO, 1952, for Admiralty, War Office and Air Ministry
Malaya: The Facts Behind the Fighting, 1952, CoI/HMSO/Colonial Office

Pamphlets covered in the text, in apparent order of preparation or publication

HMSO pamphlets are listed here in chronological order indicated by internal evidence, usually the SO code (serial) number or month of first printing when that has been revealed by the printers' codes. Occasionally, several titles were published together, without priority of issue. Dates on title pages sometimes mislead, as pamphlets were not always first put on sale within the year their printed dates suggest. Non-HMSO pamphlets present more difficulty, and have generally been listed here in accord with their title page dates, when shown.

1939
National Service
How Hitler Made War
Assurance of Victory

1940
The Battle of the River Plate

1941
The Battle of Britain
The Schools in Wartime
The Northern Garrisons
Bomber Command
The Destruction of an Army
BBC at War
The Battle of Flanders
The Defence of Calais
Fire Over London
British Railways in Wartime
Eve in Overalls (date uncertain, but 1941 seems likely)

1942
Prisoner of War
We Speak From The Air

The Saga of San Demetrio
They Sought Out Rommel
The Highland Division
Air-Sea Rescue
The Abyssinian Campaigns
Ark Royal
His Majesty's Minesweepers
Bomber Command Continues
Transport Goes to War
The Campaign in Greece and Crete
Front Line
One of Our Aircraft is Missing
Coastal Command

1943
East of Malta, West of Suez
The Battle of Egypt
Roof Over Britain
Calling All Nations
Combined Operations
The Silver Fleet
Facts About British Railways in Wartime
Meet the US Army
Fleet Air Arm
R A M C
Over to You
The Red Army (or early 1944)
Three pamphlets re-published together in hardback in 1945 as *Three Corvettes* had first been published separately between 1940 and 1943 as *HM Corvette, East Coast Corvette* and *Corvette Command.*

1944
Airborne Invasion
The Royal Marines
There's Freedom in the Air
Manpower
British Railways in Peace and War
The Eighth Army
Tunisia

Helping the People to Help Themselves (UNRRA)
Humanity Keeps an Appointment
Drive for Freedom
The Mediterranean Fleet
The First to be Freed
Life Blood
Merchantmen at War
The Air Battle of Malta
Queen Wilhelmina's Navy
Target: Germany
Before We Go Back
The Canadian Army at War – 1: The Canadians in Britain
The Australian Army at War
The Tiger Kills
The Navy and the Y Scheme

1945
100 Facts About The United Kingdom's War Effort
The Canadian Army at War – 2: Campaign in Sicily and Italy
RAF Middle East
Atlantic Bridge
Ocean Front
Arctic War
It Can Now Be Revealed
By Air to Battle
Finito!
The United Nations Today and Tomorrow
Build the Ships
His Majesty's Submarines
Land at War
The Royal Armoured Corps
Triumph in Disaster
Petroleum at War
London Calling the World
Works of Art in Italy (1945), and further series titles in 1946
Radar – A Report on Science at War
The Road to Tokyo and Beyond
Atomic Energy

1946
The Post Office Went to War
The Effects of the Atomic Bombs at Hiroshima and Nagasaki
Merchant Airmen
The Aircraft Builders (dated 1947, but on sale in 1946)
How Britain Was Fed in Wartime
The Battle of the Atlantic
Among Those Present
The Tiger Triumphs
The Campaign in Burma

1947
Friends in Need
The Protection of the Treasures of Art and History in War Areas
British Coaster
Charting the Seas
The Metropolitan Police at War
Science at War

1949
R.O.F. – The Story of the Royal Ordnance Factories
War and Archaeology in Britain
Berlin Airlift

1950
A Future In It

1952
Our Men in Korea
Malaya: the Facts Behind the Fighting

1994
Flying Bombs Over England

Other works, for further reading

Chapter 1

Ministry of Morale, Ian McClaine, George Allen & Unwin, 1979
Pioneers! O Pioneers!, Hilary Saunders, Macmillan, 1944

Chapter 2

Mission Completed, Air Chief Marshal Basil Embry, Methuen, 1957
The Blossoming World, H E Bates, Michael Joseph, 1971 (last few pages)
The World in Ripeness, H E Bates, Michael Joseph, 1972
Home and Away, John Pudney, Michael Joseph, 1960

Chapter 3

Ack-Ack, General Sir Frederick Pile, Harrap, 1949
Fanfare for a Tin Hat, Eric Linklater, Macmillan, 1970

Chapter 5

America Comes Across, Ian Hay, Hodder & Stoughton, 1942
The People's War, Angus Calder, Jonathan Cape, 1969

Generally

Propaganda in War 1939-1945, Michael Balfour, Routledge & Kegan Paul, 1979
A Bibliography of WW2 HMSO Paperbacks, A R James, 1993
WW2 HMSO Paperbacks Collectors' Guide, A R James, 1995